THE LATE
ANGLO-SAXON
ARMY

THE LATE ANGLO-SAXON ARMY

I.P. STEPHENSON

TEMPUS

Dedicated to Miriam, Marcus and Fi
With love

First published 2007

Tempus Publishing Limited
The Mill, Brimscombe Port,
Stroud, Gloucestershire, GL5 2QG
www.tempus-publishing.com

© I.P. Stephenson, 2007

The right of I.P. Stephenson to be identified as the Author
of this work has been asserted in accordance with the
Copyrights, Designs and Patents Act 1988.

British Library Cataloguing in Publication Data.
A catalogue record for this book is available from the British Library.

ISBN 978 0 7524 3141 3

Typesetting and origination by Tempus Publishing Limited
Printed in Great Britain

CONTENTS

PREFACE AND
ACKNOWLEDGEMENTS

Jim Bradbury, at the very beginning of his 1998 work *The Battle of Hastings*, notes that: 'Writing a book on the battle of Hastings for a medieval historian is a bit like reviewing one's life', and, in a way this is true. For, for any student of Anglo-Saxon history, particularly Anglo-Saxon military history, Hastings is unavoidable. Yet, despite all that, and despite all the books that I have read (and bought) on the battle, and despite always bearing it in mind (even if it were no more than at the back of my mind), when carrying out research into various aspects of ancient and medieval warfare, I have to admit that the Battle of Maldon has always held more fascination.

Why? Well, possibly because it was a more typical Anglo-Saxon battle. Possibly because (although not an unwritten about engagement) a number of aspects of the battle have been either overlooked, disregarded, or badly answered, at least as far as I am concerned. Possibly because in Byrthnoth's words at the beginning of the poem I see a continuum which stretches from the seventh century BC Greek Tyrtaeus to Colour Sergeant Bourne at Rorke's Drift and beyond to the present day.

For the poem places the battle, the English and their opponents squarely within what Victor Davis Hanson has dubbed 'the Western Way of War'. Namely the fascinating, horrendous, bloody constraint of close-order infantry combat, whose roots go back to Classical Greece and the rise of the hoplite. This is the tradition to which Anglo-Saxon warfare belongs and not, as some would have it, to a tradition based upon the anthropological study of ritualised, primitive, pre-industrialised, third-world tribes and societies.

Hastings, of course, does the same as Maldon, in terms of placing Anglo-Saxon warfare within the correct milieu. However, as has already been said, at the end of the day it comes down to personal preference, and I prefer Maldon, 'you pays your money, you makes your choice' , as the saying goes.

This current work started out, in my own mind, as a number of different, concurrent, thought processes. Firstly, I wanted to answer all of those questions about Maldon that had been going around my mind, on and off, for more years than I care to remember. Secondly, it allowed me to tackle a particular bête noire, namely the interpretation of heriots as jam spread too thinly over bread. It also gave me the opportunity to study in detail the changes in military equipment, and the reasons behind said changes, from the early to the late Anglo-Saxon period. And, of course, it allowed me to look at the campaign of 1066 and examine the reasons behind the fall of Anglo-Saxon England.

In the writing of this, as in all my previous works, a great debt of thanks is owed to Peter Kemmis Betty. Many thanks are due to Miriam Daniels for yet more superb drawings and paintings. All of the drawings and paintings in this work are by Miriam Daniels, all of the photographs were taken by myself, unless otherwise specified. Many thanks are also due to Fi and Ian Mayes, and my god-children Catriona and Ross for providing me with a peaceful place where I could write and relax. Thanks are also due to my parents and to my friends for much help and support, particularly to Tara, but also to Heinrich Härke, Lindsay Allason-Jones, Richard Underwood, Karen Dixon, Phil Clark, Paul Mullis, Ian Pain, Alex Croom, Bill Griffiths, Marcus Daniels and John Hutcheson. Finally I wish to thank my daughter, Isabella, for not being too distracting and to thank Susan, my driver, for taking me especially to Maldon, but also to Sutton Hoo.

I.P. Stephenson
Reading 2006

GROUND FLOOR

The two galleries her...
hibitions (these chang...
prove popular - pick up
leaflet at Reception.)
Shop and take a look...
ing works from our pe...
with contemporary ex...
up, or take the lift fr...
second exhibition gal...

FIRST FLOOR

The *Geology & Wildli*...
the most impressive
fossils in the world.
Archaeology Gallery,
Water Newton Silve...
relics from Roman, M...
times.

SECOND FLOOR

Bone and straw mar...
leonic prisoners-of-...
Norman Cross Galler...
site in 1797, so the ...
in existence, dates ...
The *Social History* ...
industrial and econo...
aspects of education...
tains objects some ...

We hope y...

About the building...

This beautiful building is one
of the finest examples of
Georgian architecture in the
city. It dates from 1816,
when it was built as the
private residence of Squire
Cooke, magistrate of Peterborough, and his family.

After his death, the mansion was acquired by the
3rd Earl Fitzwilliam, and became the City Infirmary. During The Great War, a mortally
wounded Anzac soldier was brought to the
infirmary, where he later died. His tragic story
has inspired a local legend — it is said his ghost
still haunts the stairwells! The building became
the city's museum. In 1939, the Art
Gallery extension was added, but due to the war,
did not house its first exhibition until 1952.
Many original features are still evident inside,
including magnificent pillars, panelled doors and
intricate cornices.

Museum trails for children...

During special events, for our younger visitors, we
have a selection of entertaining worksheets to
accompany their trip around the museum. These
are on sale at reception. (Adults might find them
fun, too!)

Need any help?

If you have any questions about the collections, or
need any assistance during your visit, please ask a
member of staff and we'll do our best to help.

Want to know more...

... about Peterborough and the surrounding region?
Our publication, *The Story of Peterborough,* is
available from Reception, currently at a sale price
of £1.00.

www.peterboroughheritage.org.uk

REGISTERED MUSEUM

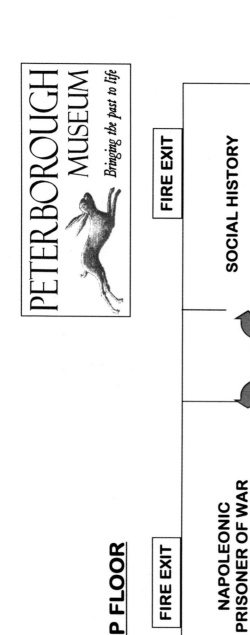

PETERBOROUGH MUSEUM
Bringing the past to life

TOP FLOOR

FIRE EXIT

FIRE EXIT

NAPOLEONIC
PRISONER OF WAR
CRAFT WORK

SOCIAL HISTORY

LIFT

FIRST FLOOR

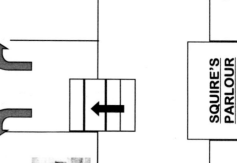

WILDLIFE

SQUIRE'S
PARLOUR

VICTORIAN
STREET / SHOP

FIRE
EXIT

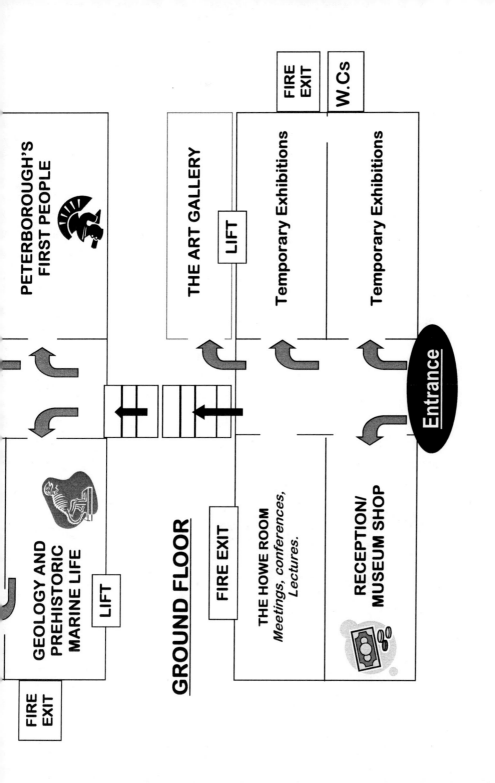

GROUND FLOOR

PETERBOROUGH'S FIRST PEOPLE

THE ART GALLERY

LIFT

Temporary Exhibitions

Temporary Exhibitions

FIRE EXIT

W.Cs

GEOLOGY AND PREHISTORIC MARINE LIFE

LIFT

FIRE EXIT

FIRE EXIT

THE HOWE ROOM
Meetings, conferences, Lectures.

RECEPTION/ MUSEUM SHOP

Entrance

1ouse our temporary ex-
regularly and always
ur *Events & Exhibitions*
rowse in the *Museum*
the *Art Gallery,* contain-
1anent collection along
bitions. Follow the stairs
1 the Art Gallery or the
y.

Gallery houses one of
1ections of marine reptile
the refurbished
scover the impressive
nd other interesting local
ieval and Anglo Saxon

try items made by Napo-
are on display in the
The depot opened on the
ection, one of the largest
< over two hundred years.
ery traces the region's
development, as well as
1d entertainment and con-
ors may find familiar!

enjoy your visit!

PETERBOROUGH
CITY COUNCIL
COMMUNITY SERVICES

PETERBOROUGH
MUSEUM
Bringing the past to life

Peterborough is a thriving modern city set against a rich heritage and surrounded by contrasting landscapes. The city owes its origins to its famous historic Cathedral that is situated right in the heart of what is now the city centre.

At the Museum & Art Gallery, we have built up an exciting picture of the region's development — from ancient marine reptiles to its modern commercial growth and cultural diversity.

There is a lively changing programme of exhibitions and events, many based upon the interests, art and cultures of the wide-ranging local communities.

Our unique, widely renowned permanent collections include exquisite items made by Napoleonic prisoners-of-war, and one of the most complete plesiosaur skeletons in the world!

We hope you enjoy your visit!

CHAPTER ONE

INTRODUCTION

Heaven's Keeper, our Creator, dressed them with clothes; the Lord commanded them cover their shame with rudimentary apparel and commanded them to depart from Paradise into a more straitened existence. Behind them at the Lord's behest a holy angel with a fiery sword closed the hope-filled home of joys and pleasures, No mortal, wicked and guilty of sin, can pass by there, but the keeper has power and strength who guards for the Lord that glorious existence, precious in its privileges.

Junius Ms. *Genesis*, XVI, 941-51

Brother will fight brother and be his slayer,
brother and sister will violate the bond of kinship;
hard it is in the world, there is much adultery,
axe-age, sword-age, shields are cleft asunder,
wind-age, wolf-age, before the world plunges headlong;
no man will spare another.

Poetic Edda *Voluspa* 45

At times, when reading the writings of later commentators on the events of 1066, one gains a sense of 'that which was lost', as if a golden age had ended and that England would never be the same again. While it is true that the events of that year did, in a way, usher in a new cycle of time (our count of kings begins at 1066 and for a long time taught history took the year of the Norman Conquest as year one). Yet in crude terms the events amounted to no more than the replacement of one warrior aristocracy by another. Indeed, in 1101 those Englishmen that owed military service in the Royal Host turned out and were loyal to King Henry I in his dispute with his brother, Robert, the Duke of Normandy.

This book is about one of those military aristocracies – the losing one. Before going on to say what this current study includes, and, importantly, what it does not include (and why), nomenclature needs to be considered.

The title of this work is *The Late Anglo-Saxon Army*. However, it could equally have been called *The Army of the Late Anglo-Saxon State*. For let us be clear about this from the very beginning; we are dealing with a form of what in later centuries would be termed *Kabineteskrieg*, and we are most definitely not dealing with *volkskrieg*. Alternatively, in title terms, Bede's prescient term *English*, to describe the successor inhabitants of the Roman provinces of Britain, can also be used to describe both state and army. As indeed can the term, from Cnut onwards at least, Anglo-Danish, and bearing this in mind, both the terms English and Anglo-Danish will be used, at times synonymously, alongside Anglo-Saxon, throughout the work.

Hollister's 1962 work *Anglo-Saxon Military Institutions on the eve of the Norman Conquest* contains a final chapter on 'Tactics and Strategy', in which he notes that military organisation and technique should not suffer:

> … too radical a separation … Since the necessities of battle in large measure govern the structure of the army.

Yet for all that Hollister does not, in his own words, 'treat in any detail' the Anglo-Saxon art of war. Nearly thirty years later in 1989, Hooper, in a short paper entitled, *The Anglo-Saxons at War*, comments that 'the subject of war and the Anglo-Saxons is a curiously neglected one.' Even today Hooper's conclusion still rings true, for with a few exceptions the picture remains similar to a decade ago. As for the exceptions, the use (or not) of cavalry in Anglo-Saxon England and, of course, the Battle of Hastings, have both proved perennially popular. The former in academic journals and the latter in numerous books and articles.

Military equipment has also fared well, albeit from an archaeological standpoint, with Falk's 1914 survey *Altnordische Waffenkunde* being the starting point for Germanic military-equipment analysis. The study of the military equipment of the period currently under consideration does, however, present a number of problems. The main works on the subject (Swanton on spears; Stephenson, Dickinson and Härke on shields; Ellis Davidson, Behmer, Wheeler, Oakeshott, Menghin, Leppäaho, Hoffmeyer, Petersen and Pierce on swords; and Tweddle on the Coppergate Helmet) deal primarily with the comparatively artefact-rich early Anglo-Saxon period. Swords are the exception, or rather since Petersen, Wheeler and Leppäaho are also concerned with spears and axes, it would be more accurate to say that Viking weapons are the exception. Although this, undoubtedly, stems from the fact that they fill the artefact vacuum. Tweddle's work on the Coppergate helmet stands out not only in that it spans the period from Vendel to Viking, but also because it touches on non-Germanic influences. Thus, the study of late Anglo-Saxon military equipment is reliant on a narrower than normal evidence base, and on the drawing of conclusions and parallels based upon earlier archaeological evidence (1). It is also noticeable that works on late Anglo-Saxon military equipment tend, in the main, to be not only European, but also predominantly Germanic/Scandinavian in orientation and ignore Byzantine, steppe and Islamic influences. This current work will, therefore, attempt to avoid the traps of relying too heavily on earlier and representational sources, while also endeavouring to take into account non-Germanic/Scandinavian evidence for the form, rise and adoption of what in military terms became *a la mode* in this period.

One area of Anglo-Saxon military history that has not suffered is institutional history. Indeed the study of the institutions has prospered, with works by Abels, Hollister, John and Powicke on the *fyrd*; Hill and Rumble on the Burghal Hidage; and Davies and Evans on Welsh and British military institutions respectively. These works, and particularly Abels' *Lordship and Military Obligation in Anglo-Saxon England*, which provide a coherent overview of the whole Anglo-Saxon period from the historical perspective of military institutions, are the reason that this aspect of English warfare is barely touched upon in this study. There is, I feel, no need for yet another 'new' work on this subject. This work is rather an operational study; an area of Anglo-Saxon warfare which in its turn is barely touched upon by the likes of Abels, Hollister, John etc., and as such this book is intended, in part, to go some way towards plugging Hooper's curiously neglected gap.

A final area in this work, also barely touched upon, is the Anglo-Saxon navy. Despite an excellent recent work on the subject by Pullen-Appleby, we are in many ways dealing with a misnomer when we speak of navies and sea power in this period. The terms the English navy and English sea power conjure images of wooden walls, Nelson at Trafalgar and Lord St. Vincent's hyperbolic, 'I do not say that the French cannot come. I only say that they cannot come by water.' For the period under study, at least, such images are false. Finds of warships, clearly distinct from the merchant ships of the period, have been made. However, they are not warships in the sense that we currently understand the term, i.e. they are not battleships. Rather, we should view them as described by Crumlin-Pedersen, namely, 'as swift landing craft for the transport of troops, only occasionally serving as fighting platforms.' Therefore, while warships and the navy do crop up in this study, they will appear primarily in their role as force projectors.

What then does this study contain?

1 This reconstruction, at Bede's World, of a male grave from the Norton-on-Tees Anglo-Saxon cemetery gives some idea of the information we lack for the late Anglo-Saxon period.

Chapter 2 provides a narrative military history of Anglo-Saxon England, from the beginning of the Second Viking Age through to the Norman Conquest – a period of roughly a century. It will look at the failure of Aethelred, and let us be quite clear about this, in an age when a king was seen as a war leader and shield of his people, Aethelred failed. It will examine Cnut's Scandinavian Empire (and his sons), before turning to Edward the Confessor. The succession crisis of 1066 is dealt with in the final chapter of this work.

Chapter 3 looks at the antecedents of Anglo-Saxon warfare. It examines the types of troops present in the English and Anglo-Danish hosts, as well as the range of tactics and tactical formations employed. In particular, it addresses the questions of cavalry, archers and the Anglo-Saxons. Given the nature of this chapter a degree of institutional creep is probably inevitable.

Chapter 4, *Military equipment, heriots and the complete warrior*, is, as the title implies, concerned with arms and armour. What was available, what was used, why it was adopted and what constituted the minimum level of equipment required for warfare? On this last point we will bring in, re-examine and reinterpret the evidence provided by late Anglo-Saxon *heriots*, or arms as death duty. In respect of what was available, what was known and what was used, this chapter, as well as the next, will of course look at the question of armour, the Anglo-Saxons and the Battle of Maldon.

A raid gone wrong is the subject of chapter 5. The battle fought at, or rather near, Maldon, in AD 991 has, as has already been mentioned in the preface of this work, a number of unanswered questions hanging over it. These questions concern the timing of the battle, the reasons behind each side choosing to give battle, the course of the action and the reason(s) for the English defeat. This chapter seeks to provide an anatomy of the battle and in the process answer the aforementioned questions.

Finally we turn to the succession crisis of 1066 and 'mad proceedings' – the phrase being originally applied to a different invasion of England by a different William. William of Orange, to be precise, he too invaded late in the year; later even than William the Bastard, although, if we are drawing parallels, it must be said that Harold II acted decisively and energetically unlike James II. Hastings tends to dominate the subject of late Anglo-Saxon England, in this study, however, it is dealt with somewhat piecemeal (Maldon has more of a starring role). Thus the campaign and battles (where anything can be said of them) of 1066 are dealt with in chapter 6, while the roles of English cavalry and archers in these engagements are discussed in chapter 3. The events of chapter 6 are normally referred to as the 'Norman Conquest', yet such a title presents a very limited view of all that occurred in that tumultuous year. Therefore, the subtitle, *the War of the English Succession*, is preferred.

CHAPTER TWO

MILITARY HISTORY

The main problem, or rather problems, with any attempt to write a military history of the Anglo-Saxons is that it rapidly degenerates into either a list of dates with the attached names of battles, or it becomes a political narrative. Indeed, in the late Anglo-Saxon period, which is the subject of this work, a political narrative is comparatively easy to write. Militarily, however, we can observe vignettes, snippets of information, which at times allow us to point the finger of blame (usually politically), but which all too often leave us with more questions than answers. We lack the information necessary to write a detailed military narrative and that, in part, is a result of the unsurprising fact that our sources had a different view point of the world and different priorities to our own. Maldon and Hastings are different and they are dealt with at some length at the end of this work. Even so, despite the fact that our sources are fuller for these two engagements than is normal for the period, both battles still generate a number of unanswered (possibly unanswerable) questions.

To us the Second Viking Age is explicable in socio-political terms. To the Anglo-Saxons it was explicable in terms of sin. Wulfstan, who was amongst other things Archbishop of York, explained in his now famous *Sermon of 'Wolf' to the English when the Danes persecuted them most, which was in the year 1014 from the incarnation of our Lord Jesus Christ*, that the return of the Vikings was God's judgement and vengeance upon the English for their many sins. Particularly and generally against ecclesiastical property, and specifically for that most terrible of crimes – regicide – the murder of God's anointed, who in this case happened to be King Edward, subsequently known as 'the Martyr'. Edward, the son of Edgar, was murdered on the evening of the 18 March 978 at Corfe in Dorset (*2* and *colour plate 5*).

2 Vikings! The Lindisfarne Stone. A fragment of a late ninth- or early tenth-century grave marker in the Yorkshire Museum, York.

Militarily, at one level the pressures faced by the Anglo-Saxon state at the beginning of the Second Viking Age were minor and local, and the response of necessity needed to be proportionate to the perceived threat. Equally, the state as a whole was in an invidious position. For just like their predecessors, the Imperial Roman Army, the armed forces of Anglo-Saxon England were required to defend and protect a rich, ordered polity against an increasingly successful and determined force of sea-borne raiders. Unfortunately, unlike their Roman counterparts they did not control both sides of the Channel, although they did try diplomatically to resolve this problem.

Turning to the various manuscripts of the *Anglo-Saxon Chronicle*, we see the worst deed done since the coming of the English to Britain, namely the murder of King Edward in 978. The 979 entry in the C manuscript is dominated by a portentous 'bloody cloud' and from 980 onwards, but a little way into the reign of the new king, Aethelred, we have a litany of raids. In 988 and 991 we have two English defeats and their accompanying slaughters, the first at Watchet and the second, more famous defeat, at Maldon. The list continues and the pattern remains the same. Raid and ravaging, punctuated by English defeats.

Examining the defeats is hard in specific terms. In the *Anglo-Saxon Chronicle* a manuscript entry for 1001 tells us that at Ætheling's Valley in Hampshire a battle was fought, it lists the prominent English dead and then goes on to say that, 'there were many more of the Danish killed, though they had possession of the place of slaughter.' The Danes, equally, 'had possession of the place of slaughter' later that same year at Pinhoe. In terms of the tactical formations used, the numbers involved, the presence or absence of surprise, we lack information. What we can surmise is that the English failure may well have been grounded in low morale and poor leadership, which were themselves the result of two decades of defeat and failure. High enemy and low English morale, may like the view of Norman invincibility that prevailed after Hastings, have resulted from the apparent inability of the *fyrd* to either prevent the raids or, if intercepted, to defeat the raiders.

Leadership at a local level at times appears decisive and resolute, if not always successful, with the examples of Byrhtnoth, as well as of Ulfcytel of East Anglia and Uhtred of Northumbria standing out. Although, in these cases, we are again reduced to lists of engagements and if lucky sparse details of actions. In 1006, for example, Simeon of Durham relates that Uhtred of Bamburgh raised the siege of Durham and placed the heads of the vanquished Scots on the city's ramparts in grim warning.

At a national level, however, things were different. In recent years attempts have been made to rehabilitate Aethelred II, the 'Unready'. The argument goes that he was an effective governor, legislator and administrator. Yet, at the end of the day this counts for nothing. A king was expected to drag 'away the mead benches from bands of foes' (*Beowulf*, lines 4-5), instead Aethelred's foes dragged away his mead bench:

> ... in that year [991] it was first decided tax be paid to the Danish men because of the great terror which they wrought along the sea coast. That was at first 10 thousand pounds.
>
> *Anglo-Saxon Chronicle* E manuscript

The payment of *Danegeld* remains to this day a controversial topic. At one level it was successful, at another it did no more than increase and excite the cupidity of the raiders. The payment of subsidies to potentially hostile elements beyond the frontiers of civilisation, to buy peace, to support and enhance friendly elements or to hire mercenaries (auxiliaries) was nothing new – the Romans were famous for it. The Romans, however, employed it with a carrot and stick mentality. The carrot was the cash, the stick, the might of the Imperial Roman Army.

The Aethelredian version, however, more carrot than stick. With the stick in Aethelred's case, being at times the military force and loyalty of those Vikings who had been paid with the carrot. In some ways the policy worked, Olaf of Norway was permanently bought off, and Thorkell the Tall proved loyal, Pallig, however, did not. In other ways the policy failed to protect the country. It did not stop the raids, and subsequent payments were larger. The buying of peace at national and local level (East Anglia attempted it in 1004) would have been widely known and militarily would have impacted badly on the morale of any English force.

In 1000 Aethelred campaigned in the north. The various chronicle sources tinge his endeavours with failure. As to the campaign's purpose, was the ravaging of Cumbria, Strathclyde and the Isle of Man intended as a show of strength generally, or just in the north? It is impossible to say for certain, although the latter case is more likely than the former. English military efforts reached a new nadir in 1006. Aethelred it would appear was collecting food rents in Shropshire while a Viking raiding-force based on the Isle of Wight ravaged, controlled and drew supplies and render from Wessex. As Tolkien, albeit in a work of fiction, *The Silmarillion*, noted:

A king is he that can hold his own, or else his title is vain.

Wessex was very much his own. The events of 1006 showed that Aethelred's title was vain. Equally the tenth-century achievements of the House of Cerdic were unravelling, England was beginning to look ripe for the picking.

Other initiatives both diplomatic and administrative impacted militarily on Aethelred's kingdom. His marriage in 1002 to Emma of Normandy made a degree of sense in that it closed the Duchy as a safe haven for Viking raiders. It also, as it turned out, provided him with a safe haven in 1013. Equally the 1002 St Brice's Day (13 November) Massacre can at best be described as an unsound policy. This attempt at ethnic cleansing (as it would be labelled in modern parlance) or as they saw it, the massacre of all the Danes living in the kingdom, was like the later 1572 St Bartholomew's Day Massacre, most probably successful in those urban areas where the ethnic mix was more English than Danish. In the Danelaw, the Anglo-Danish north, it is unlikely that the order was executed, and it is more likely that it resulted in the breeding of an ill name and an evil reputation for Aethelred, which would have disastrous results in 1013. It is equally questionable how easy it was to carry out such a policy even in the south of the country. Although, it does appear to have been attempted in Oxford at least (*colour plate 6*).

Aethelred's 1008 policy concerning the provision of military equipment is discussed below in chapter 4. His 1009 great fleet was a testimony to the strength and power of the English State. The fact that internal squabbles amongst the ruling elite caused it to fragment, to be partially destroyed by a storm, and most damningly, for the only part of it to see action to be against the south coast of England itself, points to weakness at the very top. Equally the construction of new *burhs* and the refurbishment of existing ones shows that attempts were made to increase the kingdom's defensive capabilities (*3*). However, like the great self-destructing fleet of 1009, such efforts came to naught.

A lack of leadership and internal divisions amongst the ruling elite – which led to a lack of trust and a failure to co-operate – combined to produce a lack of a coherent defence policy, which reaped its rewards in the events of 1013. The lack of a coherent strategy comes across in the fact that the 1008 legislation, the 1009 fleet, the building and refurbishment of *burhs*, all appear as one offs, seemingly unconnected to the successful application of force. While resistance, such as that in East Anglia in 1004, against Swein of Denmark, was co-ordinated at a local level. It is true that at first the raiding problem was a local problem and needed to be dealt with at a local level. However, by 1004 the problem was national and needed to be dealt with national sources. However, at this higher level resistance was non-existent and all too often raiding-armies (as the Anglo-Saxon Chronicle calls them) appear to have over-wintered in England unimpeded by the royal host.

3 Portchester, Hampshire. The 'Watergate' near the centre of the picture may well date to the eleventh century, when the site was a thegnly residence.

England was finally picked in 1013 by Swein of Denmark, whose successful campaign of conquest owed as much to the size and quality of his army (*4 and colour plates 7 and 8*), as to English failures both political (the internal squabbles, intrigues, *coups* and murders) and military (the inability to either stop, defeat or deter the raiders). The political failures of the English State stemmed in part from Edgar's early death, while military failure had been the pattern since 980. However, both were so much a part of Aethelred's kingship that he cannot, and indeed should not, escape blame. As king he was ultimately responsible for the safeguard of his realm. Swein's initial attempt to land at Sandwich failed, he rapidly moved his fleet north to the Humber and the friendlier Anglo-Danish north, which quickly submitted and took him as king. As a result of this shrewd move his next advance south, this time overland, succeeded, and the south of the kingdom followed the north's lead. London resisted, but Aethelred's failure to take the field and his subsequent flight to Normandy made further resistance futile.

4 A part of the reconstructed rampart of a late tenth-century Danish fortress of Fyrkat. Built during the unification of Denmark, this and similar fortresses show the growing power of the Kings of Denmark.

Swein's sudden death on the 3 February 1014 led to what can only be described as an unexpected military highpoint in Aethelred's career. Invited back, but on conditions, Aethelred and his host caught Cnut, Swein's son and successor in England, at unawares and unable to gather his strength. Cnut and his Danish forces fled leaving their English supporters to be "raided and burned and killed" (*Anglo-Saxon Chronicle* E ms. 1014) by Aethelred's men. Such a punishment, of his own people, may seem harsh, it was, however, at the time the price that was paid for being unsuccessful in treason. For Aethelred the success and the reprieve were temporary:

> No prince in the world more favoureth his subjects than I do you, nor no subjects or commons more love and obey their sovereign lord than I perceive you do me, for whose defence my treasure shall not be hidden, nor, if necessity require, my person shall not be unadventured.

From Henry VIII's 1545 Christmas Eve speech at the prorogation of Parliament, taken from Hall's *Chronicle* (quoted in Starkey 2000: *Elizabeth: Apprenticeship*)

Medieval monarchy was martial and the defence of the realm took precedence; the king, even as late as the Tudor period, was expected to take the field against a foreign invader. Henry VIII understood this, Aethelred II it would appear did not. Beowulf as an old man went alone into the dragon's den because he saw it as his duty as king to protect his people from all threats. While this ideal may today be seen as an extreme example, it must be remembered that the poem which starts with Scyld Scefing and with Beowulf's last fight, death and funeral, provided a behavioural model to aspire to. Aethelred, by his failure to join his army in 1016 (the army expected his presence and ceased to exist without him), and by his failure to take the field against Cnut, fell far short of expectations, and it is an indelible stain on his character. Excuses of old age and ill health will not wash. Kings, even though blind, have still fought in battles. The requirements of heroic leadership and the warrior ethic in a martial aristocracy and society were undoubtedly hard and unremitting in their tolerance of failure, and kings such as Aethelred II and Edward II who have failed to live up to such standards have been harshly judged, and rightly so. Such men were expected to lead and if need be die from the front, failure to do so, or as it has been portrayed, reluctance to do so on Aethelred's part, damned both his kingdom and his reputation.

The reign of Edmund 'Ironside' was short but active, and stands in marked contrast to that of his father's. Certainly, he was still plagued with internal political problems; militarily, however, he took the field. Again we return to the old problem of sketchy or non-existent details and simple lists of engagements.

In organisational and administrative terms the ease and ability of Edmund to raise armies points to the impressive institutional structures of the Late Anglo-Saxon State. Edmund also seems, from the D manuscript of the *Anglo-Saxon Chronicle*, to have used his forces well and successfully. However, other than the fact that he engaged in a mounted pursuit when driving the Danes into Sheppey, tactical details are lost to us. The Danes, during their siege of London in the same year, appear to have employed circumvallation, and warships as platforms from which assaults on riverside fortifications could be launched. We have no record of the English employing the same techniques, although there is no reason why they could not in similar circumstances have followed, or copied, the Dane's example. Edmund's last great battle, Ashingdon, was lost through treachery, and that is all that can be said of it. As for the stability of his subsequent treaty with Cnut, whilst it is unlikely to have lasted, it was in the event never put to the test. Edmund died on the 30 of November 1016 and Cnut succeeded to the whole kingdom (5).

5 Cnut, from the New Minster (Winchester) Register, British Library *Ms. Stowe* 944 f6r.

The mismanagement and unrealised potential, respectively, of the previous two reigns did not occur under Cnut. Although, it is likely that had he lived longer himself his great creation would have partially unravelled before his eyes. As it was, Cnut – who became more English than the English – stands as one of the most successful of medieval monarchs and certainly as the most successful Viking ever, for he created what was in effect an empire. Ruling all of England from late 1016, he inherited Denmark in 1019, conquered Norway in 1028 and even ruled parts of Sweden.

Cnut's conquest of Norway was made possible by his inheritance of Denmark and by his marriage to Emma of Normandy, Aethelred's widow. The marriage was probably in part intended to reassure the English by creating a feeling of continuity with the past, and partly in order to revive, or renew, the Normandy alliance. The former territory provided a secure launch-pad, while the latter alliance helped to secure his southern flank. Equally the wealth and manpower of his two kingdoms were instrumental in the realisation of Cnut's grand design. Thus, ironically, we see in 1025 (according to the E manuscript of the *Anglo-Saxon Chronicle*) Englishmen fighting alongside Danes against the Swedes, while in 1028 (again *Anglo-Saxon Chronicle* E ms.) men and ships from England were used by Cnut to take Norway (*6*).

Despite at times long absences by Cnut, civil war did raise its ugly head in England. This felicitous state of affairs undoubtedly resulted from the ruthlessness exhibited by Cnut at the beginning of his reign and from the loyalty of the men he appointed to rule the four great earldoms that he created, of whom Godwin, Earl of Wessex, was both the most famous and the most successful (but again we stray into the realms of political history). Cnut's other great military success, or rather creation, the housecarl, is discussed elsewhere in this work. Within the British Isles beyond England Cnut seems to have waited until 1031 (*Anglo-Saxon Chronicle* D and E mss.) before attempting to, and successfully gaining hegemony over the north of the island. In the campaign of that year, the *Anglo-Saxon Chronicle* E manuscript tells us (although we again lack details) that:

> [Cnut] went to Scotland, and Malcolm, the king of Scots, submitted to him – and two other kings, Mælbeth and Iehmarc.

Cnut died on the 12 November 1035 and was buried at Winchester. As is all too often the fate of great kings: he was succeeded by nonentities. Harold I Harefoot, Cnut's son by his first wife (or concubine, depending upon how one chooses to read the sources), is most famous for the *cause célèbre* which resulted from his murder of Alfred, the son of Aethelred II. Harefoot avoided a civil war in 1040 with his 1035 rival for the throne, Harthacnut, by the simple expedient of dropping dead.

6 Strategic mobility – an English warship on the Bayeux Tapestry, or rather from the nineteenth-century copy of the Tapestry in Reading Museum.

Harthacnut, who as the son of Emma of Normandy and Cnut, ruled Denmark first as regent for his father and then in his own right, had claimed England in 1035. He was unable to press his claim at that time as his hands had been tied by his attempts to control Norway. It was only in 1039 that Denmark and Norway, which had regained its independence, reached agreement. Harthacnut was finally free to exert his rights in England. His planned invasion, for he had gathered a great fleet, never took place, for the sudden death of his rival allowed him to obtain the kingdom unopposed. Harthacnut's short reign is reconstructable in political if not military terms. His death in 1042 saw the return of the House of Cerdic, for he was succeeded by his half-brother, Edward, the son of Emma of Normandy and Aethelred II.

The long reign, possibly to his contemporaries, the surprisingly long reign of Edward allows us to again draw up a list of engagements. We of course lack tactical information for the battles fought between 1042 and the king's death in the first days of 1066. We do, however, possess enough snippets to at least gain an insight into certain aspects of the operational art and strategic thinking employed in this twilight period of Anglo-Saxon history.

Thus in the almost-civil-war of 1052 we see that staple of medieval warfare – seaborne raiding and ravaging. The warships of the period provided strategic mobility (in fact that was their primary function), while the raiding was used to try to undermine the enemy's morale and political position (in this case the King's) by demonstrating that they could not safeguard either their own land or people. We also tactically, and in the face of the enemy in 1052, see the riverine use of warships to outflank or encircle an enemy position. Strategic mobility and speed of movement were all important factors in the hegemonic warfare of Edward the Confessor, as indeed was the element of surprise. Although, these factors should not be viewed as being confined to this period, rather they should be viewed as staples of Anglo-Saxon warfare.

Edward appears in our sources, leading fleets, and armies, as well as enjoying that most aristocratic of sports – hunting. Edward was thus in some respects the model of warrior kingship. Yet in the wars fought to reassert England's dominant position within Britain he delegated, handing over command of his armies to senior nobles. Despite the delegation of power his reputation has not suffered, partly as a result of his believed piety (he is after all known as the 'Confessor'), partly because his reign in this respect can be contrasted favourably with that of his father's, and also because the tumultuous events of 1066 have at times tended to eclipse not only his reign but also most of the history of the Anglo-Saxon period.

Speed and surprise appear as key elements in Harold's 1062 attack on Gruffydd ap Llewelyn, King of Gwynedd. Harold's target seems to have been the king himself, who fled before him. The Earl of Wessex, therefore, had to content himself with economic warfare; burning Gruffydd's manor, ships and equipment. Harold's 1062 raid, it is worth noting, smacks very much, in terms of similarity of intent, of Ecgfrith's disastrous 685 Nechtanesmere campaign. Thus the factors which we may be tempted to associate with the late Anglo-Saxon period more probably applied to the period as a whole. Before moving finally onto Siward in Scotland and Harold and his brother, Tostig, in Wales, it is worth noting that Earl Ralf and the subject of Anglo-Saxon cavalry are discussed in detail in chapter 3.

In finally dealing with the problem of Gruffydd in Wales and of re-imposing English dominance over its northern neighbour; it appears the same type of combined operation have been used. In 1054 Siward, Earl of Northumbria, led an army and a fleet against Macbeth of Scotland, while in 1063 Harold led a fleet, and Tostig (who was now the Earl of Northumbria) a land force against the King of Gwynedd. The army was intended to seek out, bring to battle and destroy its opposite number, while the fleet was designed to spread terror by raiding and harrying the enemy's coastal settlements. The fleet was also designed to raise the real possibility of a further major troop landing to the rear of the enemy's main force – trapping it in a pincer movement. In the event both campaigns were successful. Siward defeated a Scottish host which included, according to Florence of Worcester, a contingent of Normans, while Harold and Tostig received the submission of Wales. Gruffydd again fled from the English, but to no avail, he was killed by his own people on account of all the trouble he had caused. His head was presented to Harold.

Edwards the Confessor died on 5 January 1066, and Harold II Godwinson succeeded to the kingdom.

CHAPTER THREE

RITUALS, UNITS AND TACTICS

And yet the Greeks are accustomed, as I have learned, to wage war in a most thoughtless manner because of their lack of sense and skill. Whenever they declare war on one another, they search out the finest and most level area they can find. Then they have their battle there. The result is that the victors suffer great losses. As far as the losers, well I can't even begin to speak about the losers; they are totally destroyed. Surely, they ought to settle their differences by using heralds or messengers, since they speak the same language, or in any way rather than by fighting. If they really must come to blows, they ought to discover what is most disadvantageous to their opponent, and so conduct their fighting to that end.

Herodotus, 7.9.2b-g

All warfare is to some degree ritualistic. The rituals of Aztec warfare demanded the taking of noble captives. Captivity did not, however, lead to ransom and freedom, rather it led to their subsequent sacrifice, they were bent over the *chacmool* at the great temple of the war-god Huitzilopochtli in Tenochtitlán, and their hearts were cut out with an obsidian knife. The rituals of Western warfare are no stranger and just as, if not more, bloody. During the Battle of Fontenoy, 11 May 1745, the commanding officer of the First Foot Guards, Lt. Colonel Lord Charles Hay, walked out between the opposing lines, he drank a toast, shouted a taunt and then proceeded to salute the French guards facing him. His regiment then fired a tremendous volley and advanced against the enemy, smashing through the French line. The beginning of this episode was subsequently commemorated in a painting by Philippoteaux.

Rituals differ. The Aztecs had very precise rules concerning combat, violence to the human body and the conduct of warfare. The armies of Fontenoy, like Herodotus' Greeks, had rules and rituals, but such conventions as they had were concerned with peripheral aspects of warfare. To the Greeks and their successors, battle was amoral; it was ruled by military necessity and as a consequence was lethal.

Where then does Anglo-Saxon warfare fit? Did the Anglo-Saxons engage in different types of warfare? Ritual warfare? Non-ritual warfare? War as play?

The short answers to these questions are that firstly Anglo-Saxon warfare belongs with Western warfare. The English did indeed engage in different types of warfare, but it was the warfare of pitched battles between close-order infantry, and of mounted and seaborne raids. It was thus non-ritual because they did not indulge in ritual warfare or war as play as such. The ritual aspects were, like Lord Charles Hay at Fontenoy, or Nelson wearing his decorations at Trafalgar, concerned with show, display and the heroic ideal.

Part of the problem with attempts to understand warfare in Anglo-Saxon England is that although the origins are to a certain extent obvious, being derived from the *Germania* of Tacitus and from Scandinavia, the explanation and interpretation of the evidence is usually (and incorrectly) based upon prehistoric and anthropological studies, rather than from ancient Greek and Roman sources. Thus, rather than turning to primitive, pre-industrial, third-world tribes and societies in order to seek explanations for the evidence we have, instead we should turn to the Greek world. For, strange as it may seem, the single most defining ideological event in Anglo-Saxon warfare came at Marathon in 490 BC, with the triumph of the Greek hoplites over the barbarian Persians, and to this event we will return in due course.

What has been dubbed the 'Western way of war', namely the bloody constraint of close-order infantry combat, did not spring into life fully armed like the goddess Athene, rather it went through a number of key stages. The first, at the end of the eighth century BC being the introduction of the hoplite panoply. The second stage, in the late seventh century BC, and articulated in the poetry of Tyrtaeus, saw the hoplite become solely concerned with hand-to-hand combat. The Persian Wars, 490 BC and 480-479 BC, saw the ideological triumph of the hoplite and his style of warfare. While the conflicts of the Peloponnesian War (431-404 BC) and of the fourth century BC saw the final stage of development, namely, hoplites in regimented formation and strictly separated from other types of troops. The Anglo-Saxons did not go through these stages, there was no need, they were merely the inheritors of the system. However, an examination of the stages will help to place Anglo-Saxon warfare in its true context.

The hoplite panoply and its use, if different in detail, was the same in basic form and function as that carried by an Anglo-Saxon warrior. Although, this is hardly surprising as the Greek model was the archetype. Thus, in both cases we see a circular shield (approximately 1m in diameter), a long thrusting spear, a slashing sword, and a helmet, with body armour at times also being worn.

The writings of Tyrtaeus and Plutarch help to define, articulate and provide a philosophical underpinning to the hoplite's adoption of hand-to-hand combat. Equally the strength and success of this thought process and the system it delineated comes across in the fact that the words of Plutarch and Tyrtaeus are echoed and repeated in Anglo-Saxon and Carolingian sources, which are themselves describing the warfare of their own day, yet they are the same because the type of combat was the same.

Thus Byrhtnoth's exhortation, in the *Battle of Maldon* lines 20-21, to his men to 'hold their shields properly, firmly with their fists, and not to be afraid', is not materially different to 'fear ye not the multitude of men, nor flinch, but let every man hold his shield straight towards the van', which was penned by the poet Tyrtaeus in the seventh century BC. Similarly the laws of the Salian Franks mirrors the *Moralia* of Plutarch, for in the latter the Spartans disgraced 'those who throw away their shields' (*Moralia* 220A), while in the former case, although the same action still brought disgrace, equally a severe fine was imposed upon anyone falsely accusing another of shamefully discarding their shield in flight. The reason for the shame in both cases lies in the fact that the shield was carried for 'the sake of the whole line' (*Moralia* 220A).

Marathon, even by the time Herodotus came to describe the battle, had been mythologized into an ideal. It had become the model hoplite attack, and yet even though it was not so, the thought of it, the idea of it as such, is and was more important than the reality. The psychological ripples of the battle are still felt today and were very much in evidence in the warfare of Anglo-Saxon England. Marathon stands as one of the foundation stones of the Western way of war precisely because of the power of the hoplite myth of the battle. The battle not only came to represent a physical triumph, particularly for the Athenians, it was also more importantly seen as an ideological triumph demonstrating the superiority of civilised close-order hoplite infantry over the other, namely barbarian methods and forces. The dead of Thermopylae merely served to reinforce the lessons of Marathon.

The final stage in the development of the hoplite occurred in the years leading up to and during the Peloponnesian War. The rise of light infantry (javelineers, archers and slingers) and cavalry during that great conflict led to the hoplite finally becoming solely a spear- and shield-wielding heavy infantryman who fought in a block separate to his lighter armed compatriots. The task of these new, light troops was to protect the flanks of their 'battle winning' phalanx.

The same pattern existed in Anglo-Saxon warfare, with light troops occupying a peripheral role. Horsemen, where deployed, were confined to the flanks or more usually used in pursuit, while javelineers were most probably youths – albeit of the correct rank and social status – who gained their first experience of war engaged in between the lines skirmishing.

The connection between Tyrtaeus, Plutarch and Early Medieval warfare is easy to both see and ascertain. Indeed Tacitus provides a confirmatory mid-point in his *Germania* (his description of the peoples and cultures of Germany beyond the frontier). For according to Tacitus (*Germania* 6) the strength of the Germans lay in their infantry, who fought in a body, in formation, with spear and shield, and where 'to have abandoned one's shield is the height of disgrace; the man so shamed cannot be present at religious rites, nor attend a council: many survivors of war have ended their infamy with a noose.' Equally, the hoplite panoply, although different in detail, was essentially the same as that carried by the Anglo-Saxon warrior. Whilst it remains true that the English elite, like their continental counterparts, trained and were able to fight as both horse and foot, it is correspondingly true that their strength and main mode of fighting was on foot as close-order heavy infantry, and in that respect they were no different to the Greeks, Macedonians, Romans, and of course the Germans of Tacitus.

As for the connection between the Persian and Peloponnesian Wars and Anglo-Saxon England, well that connection, those connections lie with, and are concerned with success, the passage of time and spheres of cultural interaction. The Persian Wars, in victory and defeat, saw the psychological triumph of hoplite tactics, for it confirmed in the minds of the Greeks the superiority of their system over that of other lesser barbarian ones. This belief, which was actually well founded, led not only to the continuance and development of this form of warfare amongst the Greeks themselves, but also to its adoption by the Macedonians, and most notably the Romans, who were, more than anyone else, responsible for the spread of the system to the German and Scandinavian tribes living beyond the frontiers of the Empire. The lines of cultural diffusion that we take from the Persian Wars apply equally to the Peloponnesian War. The segregation of troop types, and the starring role of infantry, came in many ways to their fruition in the Imperial Roman Army. The same army which, over the centuries, fought, as well as recruited and trained the German tribes beyond the borders of Rome, and in the process passed on the Greco-Roman tradition of warfare.

It is thus hardly surprising that we see the Germans in Tacitus behaving in the same way as the Spartans before them, or for that matter the Salian Franks after them. Nor should we be surprised by the problems caused by either Saxon pirates (Ammianus XXVIII.5) or by the Germanic tribes who opposed Julian at Strasbourg in 357, for the only thing truly deadly to a Western army is another Western army.

The English thegn was (throughout the whole of the Anglo-Saxon Period) a close-order infantryman. But what did that mean in practise? What types of formation were used and what exactly were the roles of cavalry and archers in English warfare?

The earliest Anglo-Saxon literary sources, such as Bede and Eddius Stephanus, although they may record the fact that battles occurred, provided no information on the deployment of troops and merely confine themselves to recording who won and who lost. The later sources, however, do at least name and to some extent describe tactical formations and it is from these that any understanding of Anglo-Saxon battlefield formations must start.

The heroic poems *Beowulf* (lines 3117-8), *The Battle of Maldon* (lines 102, 242 and 277), and *The Battle of Brunanburh* (line 5), all describe armies as being drawn up for battle in a formation known as a 'shield wall'. The shield wall is also mentioned in Asser's *Life of King Alfred* (37) and, of course, in the *Anglo-Saxon Chronicle* entry for 937. In none of these cases is the shield wall actually described in detail, nor indeed should these sources be expected to provide such a description, as they are neither military manuals nor, for that matter, are they written for an audience ignorant of the subject matter.

What then was a shield wall? The word is rather Germanic, Anglo-Saxon even. Possibly a better word, given that the close-order Anglo-Saxon infantryman is being equated to the classical Greek hoplite, is phalanx. Equally, the *Strategikon* (XII.A.7, XII.B.14, XII.B.16 and XII.B.24) and the anonymous Byzantine treatise on *Skirmishing* (9, 10, 14, 18, 19 and 22) both use the term *foulkon*, which they see as being Germanic in origin – thus we are back to the shield wall. While Vegetius in his *Epitoma Rei Militaris* (II.17) states that "When battle commences the heavy armament stands like a wall." The fact that Anglo-Saxon warfare derived from the Greeks and the Romans (who also built on Greek foundations), means that terms such as shield wall, phalanx and *foulkon*, are, or rather should, to some extent be viewed as synonyms. But what *exactly* was a shield wall?

Modern interpretations tend to see it as a line of men whose overlapping or interlocking shields created a solid barrier or *wall* of shields. Is this interpretation correct? The simple answer is no. Firstly, this interpretation is guilty of taking a poetic term far too literally, and creating a wall of shields. Part of the reason for this, and one of the reasons why this interpretation has gained common currency, derives from the fact that writers in the Anglo-Saxon period, wishing to display their erudition, incorrectly used the Latin word *testudo* (they failed to grasp the precise military meaning of the word) for the old English term *bordweall*.

The problem, or the interlocking shields interpretation, has been further exacerbated (or given credence) by two very well known sources connected with the Battle of Hastings – namely the Bayeux Tapestry and William of Poitiers.

The Bayeux Tapestry does indeed show a shield wall of overlapping shields. However, the scene is implausible, for the troops are so closely packed together that their weapons, particularly their double-handed battleaxes, are rendered unusable. Rather the scene on the Tapestry should be read as simply representing a large number of troops in close-order. Equally, William of Poitiers statement that the English 'were so densely massed that the dead could scarcely fall' should be read in the same light. If taken literally it becomes as ludicrous as a literal belief that the French dead at Agincourt lay piled 'higher than a man'. The final part of the problem lies in the fact that in the Germanic world the shield was a very high status object and thus it is unsurprising that the word, the object, was used to describe an important formation.

Again the question, what then was the shield wall? The answer is really quite simple, and was hit upon quite some time ago (but subsequently largely ignored):

> [It] is of course merely a poetical expression for a wall-like line of shielded men. It has nothing to do with interlocking shields.
>
> Sir Charles Oman 1924, *A History of The Art of War in the Middle Ages Volume One: 378-1278 AD*, p.71 fn.1

In this definition Oman is, however, merely echoing Vegetius (*Epitoma Rei Militaris*, II.17) who stated that in battle the heavy infantry:

> ... stood *so to speak like a wall of iron* [my italics], fighting it out.

The formation was a fighting formation, it merely looked like a wall, as indeed is shown both on Trajan's Column (scene LXX) (7) and in the fifth century Vatican Vergil (Folio 66v.). Equally, it could be described as a 'spearwall', and certainly if this term were used then our understanding would be different.

Thus, Anglo-Saxon warriors, like their earlier counterparts, stood, as Vegetius tells us, wall-like, but they fought and killed primarily, as Herodian (IV.10.3) points out, with a spear. *Wall* was merely a poetic way of describing a close-order formation. Indeed, the shield wall was no more static or immobile than a hoplite, or a Macedonian phalanx. For the men in a shield wall, phalanx, or *foulkon* were expected to advance, in formation, and kill the enemy. The killing, as will be seen, was done using 'fire and shock'.

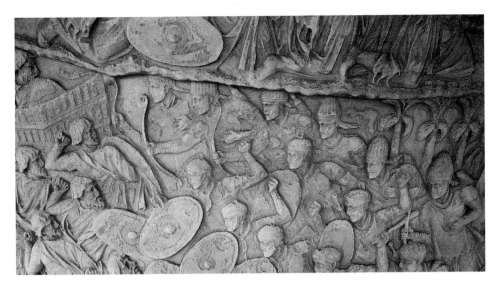

7 Infantry attacks. An auxiliary shield wall on Trajan's Column, Rome.

Before, however, going on to consider the 'face of shield wall battle' we must first turn to that other formation used by English and Viking forces in the period under study, namely the wedge. To give it its other names the *caput porcinum/caput porci* (Vegetius *Epitome Rei Militaris* III.19, Ammianus XVII.13.9), or the *svínfylking/rani* (Saxo Grammaticus *The History of the Danes* 1; Poetic Edda, *Reginsmál* 23), all of which have been translated as, or translate to, 'pig's head', pig's snout' or 'swine array'.

The best, or rather to be more accurate, the most detailed description of the formation is found in *The History of the Danes* by Saxo Grammaticus. Unfortunately, and sadly there is more than one and not only is the work thirteenth century in date, but Saxo's history is more noted for the style of his language than for the quality of his research which is poor at best. As for the Poetic Edda and the Sagas, as sources they are of little use, for besides date and quality problems, they simply provide the title of the formation without providing a description. Turning to the Roman sources, Ammianus' (XVII.13.9) *caput porci* was *angustum fronte* or narrow fronted, and that is about the limit of his description. Vegetius is more loquacious on the subject of the wedge, in book 3 chapter 9 of his *Epitome Rei Militaris*, he describes a formation 'narrower in front and broad behind', which was designed to break an enemy's line by concentrating a large number of missiles onto a portion of the opposing shield wall.

What then was a wedge? There are basically two schools of thought. The first school, simply and uncritically, follows Saxo's description of successive ranks of men in 2, 4, 8, etc. or 2, 3, 4, 5, etc. to produce a very pointy wedge.

The second, promoted by Delbrück, argues that the wedge was in fact a column of attack. Certainly if one looks at a pig or boar's head and snout (*8*) the pointy model does not fit the name, nor does it entirely match a column of attack, although the latter does provide a closer fit.

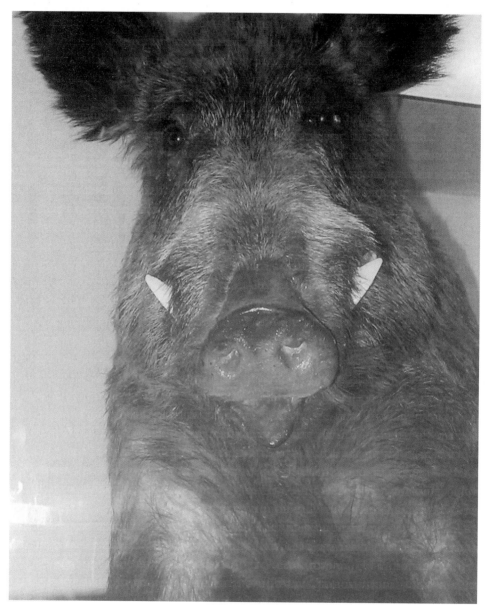

8 Front view of the decidedly flat snout of the common European wild boar. This example is on display in the Natural History Museum, London.

There is no easy solution to the problem of what a wedge actually looked like, for with all questions of this nature it comes down to a reading, an interpretation of the admittedly limited evidence.

Saxo's description, although detailed, provides for an excessively complex, probably unworkable formation. It is also true that his description does not fit with the more reliable picture painted by Vegetius. The view of the wedge in the *Epitome Rei Militaris* accords more with a column of attack. What is more the column of attack is easy to form, manoeuvre, is fast (certainly compared to advancing in line) and can break through a line (it thus fits all of the wedge's criteria). The use of columns of attack also accords with one of the rare tactical descriptions present in Anglo-Saxon literature. Asser's *Life of King Alfred* (37-9) describes how an English army attacked uphill, in two divisions, and defeated their Viking opponents. Although the English were initially drawn up in a shield wall, Asser (*Life of King Alfred* 38) goes on to state that 'when he [Alfred] had closed up the shield wall in proper order, he moved his army without delay against the enemy.' The closing up of the shield wall implies a change of formation, and this impression is further reinforced by the fact that the English moved forward 'without delay'. Advancing in line is a slow, tricky business, as the line must be constantly dressed in order to ensure that it remains straight. The evidence (Asser) thus suggests that Alfred reorganised his line into columns of attack which are far easier to manoeuvre, keep their formation without the need for constant dressing and can move (even uphill) relatively quickly. The benefits of a column are obvious, given the fact that Alfred's attack was uphill and in the face of the enemy's missiles.

Where then does all of this leave the wedge or the 'pig's head'? The phrase 'pig's head' as our Roman sources are at pains to point out, was no more than soldier's slang. We may thus be placing too much credence on an inexact description of a formation. With this in mind, it is worth noting that the same is also true of Agathias' description of the Franks at the Battle of the Casilinus River in 554. Agathias (2.8) tells us that the Frank's wedge formation 'was *like* a triangular figure *resembling* the letter delta' (italics added). Haldon in his *The Byzantine Wars* views the wedge simply as two columns of attack which 'converged at the head' forming a hollow trapezoidal formation, and in this interpretation we are probably getting close to the truth of the wedge.

Leaving aside Saxo and soldier's slang, the wedge, as a formation, makes most sense as a column of attack; a formation known for its ability to advance quickly, to be hard to completely disrupt and to have the potential to break lines. However, given the fact that we are not dealing with Napoleon's Imperial Guard, it is possible, even probable, that the formation was not parade ground neat. Thus while the front ranks (the snout?) comprising the war-leader and his housecarls (to whom we will shortly turn) maintained formation, it is equally possible that the back end of the column was not so neat and spread slightly forming a trapezoidal or pig's head shaped column.

Leaving the column or wedge to one side for the moment we return to the shield wall. The next questions we must attempt to answer with respect to the shield wall are concerned with depth and organisation. Depth has no certain answer, even turning to our Roman sources we gain no definite solution for the depth to which the Imperial Roman Army deployed. Josephus and Vegetius describe – and in the case of the latter, favour – a three/six deployment, whereas Arrian and Maurice prefer a four/eight solution. Thus, Roman infantry, and it is very likely that the Anglo-Saxons followed the same pattern, normally deployed in lines three or four ranks deep, employing deeper six or eight rank formations when facing cavalry. There was undoubtedly, in both the Roman and Anglo-Saxon worlds, no hard and fast rule concerning line depth, and the use of 3/6 and 4/8 in warfare was probably very dependant upon circumstances and the numbers involved. Although it is very unlikely that they deployed in ranks less than three deep, as such a two or one rank deep formation would lack solidity, would be easily breached by cavalry or infantry, and swiftly collapse leading to ruin and rout.

To the Greeks the right of the line was the place of honour. From what we can deduce of Anglo-Saxon and Anglo-Danish organisation it appears that the centre of the line had precedence. Although it must be admitted that the evidence for this is slight, as it is merely implied in the *Battle of Maldon* (lines 17-24) and only explicitly stated of Harold II, at Hastings, in the *Carmen de Hastingae Proelio*.

At Hastings, Harold stood amongst his housecarls. The housecarls, a creation of Cnut, have at times been seen as something new. Yet in truth Cnut's creation did not come out of a clear blue sky. Rather it was based upon the household troops (*comitatus*) of the English and Danish courts and aristocracy. The housecarls were thus probably no more than an expansion, in terms of numbers, and a formalisation, in terms of structure, of an existing and well known institution. In terms of numbers and primary function, the housecarls, from Cnut to Harold II, provided the king with a large body of full-time professional warriors. It was certainly not large enough to allow the king to fight a war without calling upon the forces of the *fyrd*, but it was of a size to provide a formidable core to any royal army. We also know from Siward's 1054 campaign in Scotland (*Anglo-Saxon Chronicle* D manuscript) that the great nobles in the realm also maintained their own force of housecarls. This of course should come as no surprise for the housecarls were no different to Byrhtnoth's hearth-troop (*The Battle of Maldon* line 24) or for that matter to Hnaef's:

... nor ever did a man's own brave companions make better payment for the white mead than his young warriors made to Hnaef.

The Fight at Finnsburg, lines 37-40

As for the organisation of the rest of the shield wall, whilst we can, in institutional terms, understand the basic tactical unit, we can only surmise with regard to the order of battle. Thus, while the *fyrd*, be it a full royal host, or an earl's army, was organised as Abel's argues along divisions based upon shires, hundreds and private sokes; the basic tactical building blocks were the contingents of the nobles, while those who owed service direct to the king being marshalled and commanded by their local sheriff. In the late, as in the early Anglo-Saxon Period, lords and their armed retainers played the main role in warfare and in the make-up of English armies. How these units were arranged when, to rephrase *The Battle of Maldon* line 22, the troops were suitably arrayed, can only be a matter of conjecture. There was undoubtedly a known order of precedence based upon social rank used to array units, possibly similar to the status system which the Greeks used to place contingents from different city states in the same line of battle and ensure that they were correctly ordered. It is possible that the higher the rank of a unit's commander, the closer to the centre of the line it was placed.

Now we should not delude ourselves into thinking that these formations that we have just described, wall and wedge, were (as some commentators have argued) late creations. The product of an impetus in the eighth century, which in actuality did not exist. Rather, (as I have already argued in *The Anglo-Saxon Shield*) the panoply of a large shield, thrusting spear and slashing sword was a constant of Anglo-Saxon warfare, and consequently so were the tactical formations that went with it. For Anglo-Saxon warfare, and for that matter its continental predecessor, was part of the mainstream – in terms of equipment, techniques and tactics – of the Western way of war, and that should not be forgotten.

We must now turn to the questions of combat, symmetry, and how these formations worked in practise.

At Marathon in 490 BC the opposing battle lines were drawn up approximately 1.5km apart and it is believed that the Greeks ran the last 200-300m. Was the extreme distance covered at a run at Marathon the killing zone of the Persian archers? Probably. If so then the same conditions did not apply in Anglo-Saxon England; for as will be seen below, archery, although it played a part in Anglo-Saxon warfare, was never of any great significance. In English warfare the killing zone had a depth of some thirty yards, or the maximum effective range of the javelin. Our sources do not tell us how this distance was crossed. The problems, for close-order infantry, in crossing a killing zone concern speed and cohesion.

For the faster a line, or shield wall, moves the more likely it is to cease being a line, to loose cohesion and be easier to break and destroy; as it would, on reaching the enemy, already possess natural gaps and tears, which could be exploited. Equally, if we add into the equation the weight of the equipment (and it must be remembered that the shield must be held out from the body in order to function correctly) that crossing too great a distance at a run would tire a warrior and reduce combat effectiveness. It is, however, probable that given 30 yards is only about as many paces, that this distance was crossed in less than a minute at a quick walking pace. Where the depth of the killing zone was greater, such as at the Battle of Ashdown in 871 where Alfred was forced to attack uphill (see Asser's *Life of King Alfred*, 37-9), a shield wall or line would not serve – thus we see the English forming columns in order to cross the distance with alacrity, without sacrificing cohesion in the process.

Shield walls worked, in general terms, by using 'fire and shock'. Even if as at Maldon the 'fire' (bows and javelins) was not that effective, it was still employed in an attempt to overcome the problem of symmetry. In *Judith* the missile attack (in this case spears) was accompanied by a huge roar, which was possibly the Anglo-Saxon version of what the Roman's termed the *barritus*. As for the reintroduction of a missile capability (the javelin) into the hoplite panoply, that was Roman in origin. The symmetry, in military terms, stemmed from the fact that in battle the arms, equipment, tactics and training were the same for the English and their opponents. Victory therefore was dependant upon other factors – morale, luck (such as the death of Byrhtnoth at Maldon), numbers, even possibly the weight of missiles failing on a shield wall prior to contact. The Battle of Hastings in 1066, was lost or won – depending upon your perspective – because the sides were asymmetrical, even so it was still not an easy victory.

The Maldon poet's emphasis of, and concentration on the spear is perfectly correct and normal, for in the shield wall when the lines met, and in the pursuit, it was the main weapon of death. For when the lines met, the killing took place at a distance of less than the length of a spear. At this stage of the fighting the spear was thrust or thrown, depending upon what target opportunity presented. However, unlike in the Early Anglo-Saxon Period, the butt-spike appears to have been little used even though the tactical situation which had created it remained. Rather, once the spear was lost or its head was broken the warrior reverted to sword or axe in order to beat down his opponent and to break the enemy's line. As to the actual mechanics of this form of combat – little can be said. They fought, they killed, and they hacked (or at least tried to) their way into the enemy's shield wall with sword or axe. For a heroic warrior aristocracy this was the epitome of their existence, what they had lived for, been bred for, and been trained to do since childhood – everything came together on the field of battle. As indeed is articulated in the Anglo-Saxon poem *Judith*:

> Swiftly then with their gleaming swords those valiant heroes made an inroad through the thick of their foes; they hacked at shields and sheared through the shield wall.

Once the lines had met, and particularly in this age of heroic leadership when commanders fought in the front rank of the shield wall, control of the battle very much ceased and events were left to take their course. Harold II at Hastings appears to have been unusual in that he may not have stood in the very front of the battle, and thus was able to issue orders and attempt to control events. Equally Hastings was unusual in that it lasted all day and in that the enemy attacked in waves, with retreats and lulls in between bouts of activity. Normally, when battle was joined the conflict was short and swift with no respite in the fighting until one side gave way. For the object, once the shield walls met, was to defeat the enemy. Defeat being achieved either by the infliction of some catastrophic event such as the death of a leader – with the death of Byrhtnoth at Maldon being the obvious example – or by the swift breaking of the enemy's shield wall, and this we may imagine is what Alfred achieved at Ashdown and Athelstan at Brunanburh, particularly as in the latter case the pursuit lasted all day, thereby implying a swift victory.

The breaking of the shield wall was important because if one side could punch a hole through the other's line, then their opponents unshielded backs would become vulnerable, their morale would in all probability collapse, and thus the enemy's line could be easily rolled-up. The whole, bloody process of creating tears and gaps by killing the enemy at close-quarters and by fighting your way into and through your opponents line was all with the sole purpose of causing the disruption, loss of cohesion and disintegration of the shield wall that you were trying to defeat. Such was how battles were won. Each side was of course trying to achieve the same ends with the same basic material – thus symmetry. Technological, or equipment solutions to the problem of symmetry were of course rapidly adopted by all sides – in this period such a solution was the broad or Danish axe (see below, chapter 4), which first appeared around the millennium and which may well have been developed and adopted partly in order to break shield walls. Its other martial use was concerned with the rise of cavalry. However, a third use was purely concerned with status and display, for a number of figures on the Bayeux Tapestry, in courtly as opposed to battlefield settings, appear without armour yet holding a broad axe as a mark of martial prowess.

Of course the alternative to the swift collapse and the catastrophic event was slow attrition, and again an obvious example presents itself. The slow haemorrhaging of the English at Hastings in 1066 meant that at the end of the day their shield wall lacked the ability, the stability, to withstand the final Norman assault.

The collapse once it occurred would have been swift and then the pursuit would have begun. Casualty figures are impossible to ascertain, the best that can be said is that in this type of warfare the loosing side usually suffers a far higher number than the victors and that the majority of a defeated sides casualties will have occurred at this stage. This is why our sources refer to such events as slaughter, for indeed a pursuit could and frequently did produce a charnel house. For a victorious English army the initial phase of the pursuit would have been on foot, but the horses would have been swiftly brought up and then the mounted phase would have begun, and this phase would have lasted until night or terrain intervened. Whether on foot or horse the spear was the ideal weapon of pursuit, as it had the edge over the sword in terms of length of reach:

> There in the dust fell the main part of the muster-roll of the Assyrian nobility, of that odious race. Few survivors reached their native land.

Judith

CAVALRY/ĒOREDGERÏD

> An earl belongs on a charger's back; a mounted troop must ride in regular array, and the foot-soldier stand firm.

Maxims I

The question of the use of cavalry in the Anglo-Saxon period has been much-debated. The argument has in the main centred around the use of cavalry in Bernicia (9) in the Early Anglo-Saxon Period, while in the late period it has tended to centre around Earl Ralf in 1055, and the Battle of Stamford Bridge in 1066. Alcock argues for cavalry warfare and his argument is in the main accepted by both Hooper and Cessford, although it is rejected by Higham. Yet, before looking at the evidence for cavalry, and before considering the effect cavalry would have had on tactics if it were used, the first question to be asked should be what is meant by cavalry?

9 A reconstruction, at Bede's World, of Yeavering in Northumbria. Of particular note is the great paddock enclosure in the background.

> The general term of Cavalry, as commonly received, comprises every description of soldiers serving on horseback.
>
> Warnery 1798, *Remarks on Cavalry*

However, Warnery, in his *Remarks on Cavalry*, also stated that cavalry had a 'regular system or method'. This point is reiterated by Delbruck in Volume IV of his *History of the Art of War*, where he argues that 'cavalry consists of tactical bodies composed of horsemen.'

Cavalry, the argument follows, although similarly equipped to the mounted warriors of the medieval period (as a whole), is fundamentally different in 'spirit, actions, and concept'. Cavalry as a tactical body has undergone a high level of drill and acts as a closely formed and controlled unit. Anglo-Saxon warriors were trained, but there is no evidence that they were drilled. In this context, then, the Anglo-Saxons did not possess cavalry. Individuals may have had the ability to fight on horseback and it is the evidence for this, and the effect that this may have had on the warfare of the day, which will be considered next.

Archaeologically, from the Early Anglo-Saxon period, there have been a number of finds of horse gear in graves, some of which also included weaponry. These finds, however, neither prove nor disprove mounted combat. Nor should anything be read into the absence of stirrups, as the stirrup is not a prerequisite of mounted combat. As to the types of weapons found in the horse burials, they are mostly high-status weapons (sword, seax and axe) although spears and shield fittings were also deposited. In terms of usage, although none of the weapons were specifically designed for mounted combat, it is also true to say that none of the weapons could not have been used on horseback for, with the single exception of the bow, all of the weapons used by the Anglo-Saxons could have been used with equal efficiency on both foot and horseback. Higham's claim that the weapons of the Anglo-Saxon were unsuitable for mounted combat is nonsensical given the fact that (to give but two examples) both the Roman cavalryman and the Norman knight fought on horseback using a long, heavy slashing sword and a leaf-bladed thrusting spear. As for the late Anglo-Saxon period we have a number of finds of stirrups, spurs, bits, as well as a part of a Viking Period saddle from York (*10* and *11*; *colour plate 9*). Equally, the ubiquitous manuscript illustrations of puttees points to a horse orientated, riding society. Puttees, contrary to popular belief, were not worn to keep the lower leg warm, rather they were an important piece of riding equipment. Today, as the photograph of my god-daughter shows (*12*), half-chaps are worn rather than puttees, but both performed the same protective function.

Representational evidence for mounted combat (*13, 14, 15, 16, 17*) is provided by the depictions of mounted Anglo-Saxon warriors on the reverse of the cross-slab at Aberlemno, Angus (Aberlemno no.2) and on Die Design 2, "Rider and Fallen Warrior", from the Sutton Hoo helmet. In the case of the Aberlemno example, Northumbrians are shown on horseback engaged in combat with both foot and mounted opponents, whilst the Sutton Hoo example depicts a warrior riding down his opponent. Both depictions show the mounted warriors protected by shields and fighting with spears or javelins; all of which is perfectly feasible, and probably represented the reality of the mounted combat of the day. The use of the javelin from horseback is an accepted method of combat and is attested from both earlier Roman sources, such as Arrian's second century work on tactics (*Ars Tactica*, 42), and later sources, such as the eleventh-century Bayeux Tapestry. Bearing this in mind, Higham's view that the use of the javelin in mounted combat 'verges on the incredible' does not stand up to scrutiny, and indeed Higham's view has been plausibly and correctly refuted by Hooper, Cessford and Rowland. Depictions of mounted combat with weapons other than the spear are unfortunately lacking, although the Repton Stone does show a single figure of a mounted warrior brandishing sword and shield.

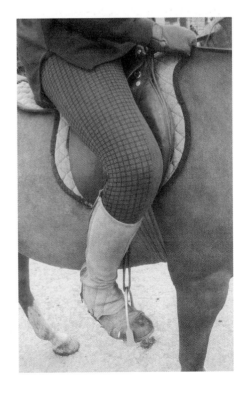

Above left: 10 Tenth- or eleventh-century brass-inlaid iron stirrups from Battersea, in the British Museum.

Above right: 11 A Viking period spur in the Yorkshire Museum, York.

Right: 12 Half-chaps as worn by my god-daughter Catriona Mayes. The modern equivalent of the Anglo-Saxon elite's puttees.

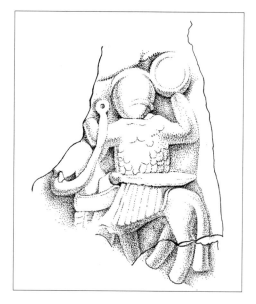

Above: 13 Die Design 2, 'Rider and fallen warrior' from the Sutton Hoo helmet.

Left: 14 The rider from the eighth-century Repton Stone.

Opposite: 15 The reverse of the Cross-Slab at Aberlemno, Angus (Aberlemno no.2).

Above left: 16 Mounted combat. A detail from the tenth-century Gosforth Cross. *Redrawn by M. Daniels from Bailey 1980.*

Above right: 17 Mounted combat. The Viking period Neston Cross, Fragment 5, Face C. *Redrawn by M. Daniels from White 1986.*

The fact that the Sutton Hoo example can be closely paralleled by symbolic depictions of cavalrymen on both Greek and Roman tombstones does not affect the validity of the scene, as the riding down of a foot soldier is an accepted method of mounted combat. However, in the case of Die Design 2, 'Rider and Fallen Warrior', from the Sutton Hoo helmet a caveat must be added. The Swedish antecedents of the helmet from mound 1 at Sutton Hoo may possibly mean that the scene depicts the realities of Swedish as opposed to Anglo-Saxon warfare, particularly in the light of Engström's argument that mounted warfare was a common part of Swedish (Vendel) warfare in this period.

The Viking-period (dated to between AD 930-1020) Neston cross Fragment 5 Face C, although it has been compared to the reverse of the cross-slab at Aberlemno, Angus (Aberlemno no.2), does not aid our understanding of mounted combat in the early Anglo-Saxon period due to the lateness of its date. Its depiction of a 'joust' is unusually early; however, leaving that aside, its value in terms of the use of horses/mounted forces in combat is in the main confined to the fact that it provides as White argues:

… further confirmation that mounted horsemen used spears.

As for the Bayeux Tapestry, the work merely serves to confirm and contextualise Harold Godwinson, and by extension the warrior elite of Anglo-Saxon England, as a part of the European mainstream in terms not only of equipment, but also in that militarily he was perfectly at home on horse or foot.

Although the literary evidence, along with a number of manuscript illustrations, points to the Anglo-Saxons using the horse as a means of transport to battle, it also supports the thesis that the Anglo-Saxons were capable of engaging in mounted combat. The primary example of the former is *The Battle of Maldon* (lines 2-3), although Eddius Stephanus' *Life of Wilfrid* (19), provides the earliest piece of evidence for a mounted force, when it describes King Ecgfrith as commanding a mounted host. Examples of the latter are provided by the *Anglo-Saxon Chronicle* entries for 937 and 1016:

All day long the West Saxons with elite cavalry pressed in the tracks of the hateful nation, with mill-sharp blades severely hacked from behind those who fled battle.

The Anglo-Saxon Chronicle A manuscript, 937

It was a riding-school exercise. Hardly breaking formation, the lancers rode down the slope through the retreating Zulus, picking their men from the ruck. The momentum of the horses spitted the warriors on the points, and as they passed, a strong outward flick of the wrist cleared the weapon, which swung back, up and forward again to point, with stained tip and dyed pennon, at the next victim.

Morris 1966, *The Washing of the Spears*

The Boeotians followed them up and cut them down – particularly the Boeotian cavalry and the Locrians, who had come up just after the rout began. The pursuit, however, was cut short by the coming on of night, and so the bulk of the fugitives escaped more easily than they would have done otherwise.

Thucydides *History of the Peloponnesian War*, bk.4 ch.7

The shadow cast by Delium is very long. Nor should this be seen as surprising, for the largest battle of the Archidamian War not only saw (as some later commentators have stated) the birth of tactics, but importantly in this current context, it saw the beginning of that most desirable of ends (for the victors at least) – the rout and pursuit by cavalry of the enemy. The period of the Peloponnesian War was a time of great invention, ingenuity and creativity, and no where was this more so than in the field of warfare. For the cavalry arm it saw an increase in its importance and a consequent rise in its battlefield role. The now mostly forgotten battle fought at Delium in November 424 BC not only saw the end of Athenian hopes to knock Boeotia out of the war, it was also witness to, on the part of the Boeotians, the first successful co-ordination of hoplites and cavalry. The result of this integration being not only the defeat of the Athenians, but a vigorous and bloody pursuit of the defeated infantry, which set the pattern for and became the ideal to be aspired to, in the future. Delium then not only showed what cavalry could achieve, it also also set one of the preconditions for the end of such a pursuit, namely the coming of night. Ulundi, in AD 1879, which stands as a direct descendant of Delium, shows another precondition for the ending of a cavalry pursuit. Here a change in terrain led the British to call a halt to, to use an idiom, the 'pig-sticking'.

The Battle of Brunanburh, another child of Delium, in AD 937 followed the model, in textbook style, of its parent. In that Athelstan and his host rapidly overthrew the enemy shield wall. The English then mounted, and bloodily pursued the vanquished enemy for as long as the daylight lasted. We are less well informed about other English mounted pursuits. In 1016 (according to the F manuscript of the *Anglo-Saxon Chronicle*) King Edmund, at some point prior to his defeat at Ashingdon, pursued Cnut's raiders. Both sides appear to have been mounted and although we cannot for certain ascertain the reason for the breaking off of the chase, it does appear that Edmund's forces were able to cut-up the enemy's rear-guard. The use and value of mounted forces in a pursuit capacity was well known to – and where possible well used by – the Anglo-Saxons. The fact that at times, as in 1055, they were on the receiving end, should be seen simply as a result of the vagaries of warfare and not as a lack of ability.

The representational evidence, apart from Aberlemno, for mounted shock tactics is limited to the two horsemen depicted on Neston Cross Fragment 5 Face C, the interpretation of which is open to discussion. Aside from Nechtanesmere in 685, which does appear (at quite an early date) to show that the English would engage infantry from horseback; we have, historically, to consider Earl Ralph and the events of 1055, and of course Harold Godwinson in Wales, Normandy and at Stamford Bridge.

We have two problems when it comes to the subject of Earl Ralph and the question of mounted warfare in Anglo-Saxon England. The first problem is Florence of Worcester, and the second problem, well that is a lack of information concerning the events of 1055. The *Anglo-Saxon Chronicle* tells us that Earl Ralph, in order to counter a force of Welsh and Irish led by King Gruffydd and the outlawed English earl, Ælfgar, assembled a great force at the market town of Hereford. The C manuscript entry for 1055 then goes on to say that:

> … before there was any spear thrown, the English people already fled, because they were on horse, and a great slaughter was made.

The D manuscript entry of the *Anglo-Saxon Chronicle* for 1055, however, states that:

> … and with a little struggle they were brought to flight, and many people killed in that flight.

The problem comes from Florence of Worcester, who although heavily reliant on the *Anglo-Saxon Chronicle* as a basic source of information, does at times – and this is one of them – add extra information, which in this instance only serves to muddy the water. For Florence tells us that in 1055:

> [Ralph] ordered the English, contrary to their custom, to fight on horseback. But just as they were about to join battle, the earl with his Frenchmen and Normans set the example of flight: the English seeing this, fled with their commander.

The entry goes on to say that the enemy pursued and slaughtered the fleeing English.

At the heart of the matter lies the question of information, or rather our lack of it. For while we can with a high degree of confidence reconstruct the political events of 1055, the same cannot be said for the events surrounding the military débâcle at Hereford. Leaving to one side, for the moment, the question of "contrary to custom", it appears from the *Anglo-Saxon Chronicle* entries that the English either panicked prior to contact and fled without striking a blow, or else they engaged the enemy; but then just after engaging, something happened which betrayed the English into retreat, flight and slaughter. Florence of Worcester, and for that matter Simeon of Durham, blamed Earl Ralph and his fellow Normans, who they say turned tail ere a blow was struck. Certainly, in that age, when heroic leadership was prized and held at a premium, the cowardly flight of the war leader and his household troop would have had a disastrous effect on the rest of the force, and would easily account for the precipitous retreat.

Indeed at Maldon in 991, the believed flight of the already dead Byrhtnoth shattered the shield wall and doomed the English to defeat.

What then of 'contrary to custom'? In a way this gloss helps explain the ease and speed of the defeat, but is it really that simple? The phrase is used by Florence and Simeon, yet their works date to the early 1100's and they rely heavily on earlier sources, particularly the *Anglo-Saxon Chronicle*, for their accounts of the events in question, and give that the various manuscripts of the *Anglo-Saxon Chronicle* do not mention this custom, it is thus possible that they may be either mistaken, have misunderstood their evidence or be simply wrong. We also do not know to which custom in particular they were referring. Certainly, the argument that has at times been advanced, that it was contrary to the custom of the *entire* English nation, does not stand even the most basic scrutiny. Thus at best we are looking at a local custom, or rather a local tactical custom. Rather the disaster at Hereford in 1055 appears to have been more a result of poor leadership, than an inability on the part of the English to engage the enemy from the back of a horse.

Harold Godwinson presents an obvious contrast to Earl Ralph the 'Timid', yet as with all aspects of Anglo-Saxon mounted warfare the subject of Harold and cavalry is by no means straightforward.

According to the D manuscript entry of the *Anglo-Saxon Chronicle* for 1063, Earl Harold led a force to Rhuddlan and although he surprised Gruffydd and burnt his hall, his quarry escaped, albeit temporarily. Florence of Worcester, expanding (yet again) upon the *Anglo-Saxon Chronicle*, states that the English force consisted of a 'small troop of horsemen'. Harold's Welsh strategy, of rapid movement and surprise, was of course repeated a few years later, when as king he marched north to York and his greatest battlefield success. It is also reminiscent of what we can glean of Ecgfrith's plan for the Nechtanesmere campaign. In the latter case, Ecgfrith (according to Eddius Stephanus in his *Life of Bishop Wilfrid* (*19*)) led a mounted host, and thus it is likely that Florence is correct and that Harold's force was also mounted. Although this is hardly surprising for two reasons. Firstly, a small fast (and therefore mounted) force was the best means of achieving Harold's end, namely that of taking the enemy at unawares in the midst of his own territory. Secondly, and to some extent obviously, all of the evidence points to the fact that English warriors rode to battle. Having said all of that, however, Harold's Welsh raid, and for that matter his rapid marches north and then south in 1066 merely show him taking full advantage of the mounted and thus potentially highly mobile nature of Anglo-Saxon armies. These events tell us nothing about the use of the horse by the English on the field of battle.

Further reinforcing the case for the battlefield use of the horse by the English, as well as confirming the place of the English within the mainstream of continental warfare, we turn to William of Poitiers and the Bayeux Tapestry.

Neither of which have any problem with Harold's participation in, or indeed his ability to participate in, William's Breton campaign.

Finally, with Harold we turn to the Battle of Stamford Bridge. In many ways the use of the horse by the English in events prior to what turned out to be the second battle of the campaign of 1066 was highly conventional in that, as with Harold's earlier Welsh expedition, it fulfilled its everyday strategic mobility role. The problem arises in that in one of the most detailed and certainly the best known description of the battle, namely that contained in the *Heimskringla* of Snorri Sturluson, the Anglo-Saxon's use of cavalry is described in such a way as to elevate it to a pivotal position, whilst at the same time sounding remarkably like a slightly later and far more famous engagement. *Heimskringla* was written in the thirteenth century, thus the criticism that is usually levelled that Snorri confused the events of Hastings and Stamford Bridge is cogent. *Heimskringla* does not, however, stand alone. Equally detailed accounts of the battle occur in the *Morkinskinna* and in the *Fagrskinna*. Unfortunately, they also date to the early thirteenth century and thus present the same transmission of information problems as Sturluson's work. Leaving these problems to one side for a minute it needs be admitted that with the exception of the English "feigned retreats", the description of the battle in these sources does not exceed the bounds of possibility. As for the use of a mounted force to pin and harass the Norwegians, this should be seen as a plausible English tactic and certainly the sort of thing that would have been known and understood by Harold, and for that matter the Anglo-Saxon military elite as a whole. The subject of the "feigned retreats" is problematic and dependant upon context. For the Byzantine version of the manoeuvre differed from the Norman. Did the English use it? Or was it a lucky battlefield occurrence given a post-facto rationalisation? Or for that matter is it a mistake in our later source material? Given the current state of the evidence it is impossible to say. As for a mounted Anglo-Saxon contingent at Stamford Bridge, it is still a possibility that a part of Harold II's host remained horsed in order to pin and contain the enemy. However, given the dearth of information in our contemporary sources little can be said other than that it remains a feasible possibility.

The evidence, such as there is, has therefore led Hooper to conclude that mounted combat took place 'mainly in skirmishes and pursuits rather than in pitched battles.'

Although Hooper does not rule out the use of mounted contingents in pitched battles, he does believe that the Anglo-Saxons usually dismounted and formed a shield wall. There is no evidence to either positively support or refute this proposition, and the use of mounted contingents in pitched battles, therefore, remains a possibility. However, given the Anglo-Saxon's obvious ability in raid, pursuit and rout and coupled with the Bayeux Tapestry's support for the fact that England's warrior aristocracy were a part of the European mainstream; it is probable that the English at times deployed tactically diverse units on the battlefield, and that cavalry (in the broadest sense of the word and remembering initial definitions) were a part of the tactical repertoire of late Anglo-Saxon armies. However, little should be read into the absence of English cavalry at the Battle of Hastings. Rather we should see this as a case of "horses for courses", or deployment to suit the tactical situation. At Hastings, surprise having failed (see chapter 6), the position from an English point of view was better suited to infantry. Equally Harold II was undoubtedly wise in not allowing any English horse to engage their, if not necessarily numerically superior, better opponents.

ARCHERY

The solitary, diminutive English bowman on the Bayeux Tapestry (*18*) has tended to beg the question, particularly in the light of the success of Norman archery at the battle – where were Harold's archers? Yet as Manley begins to approach in his paper, *The Archer and the Army in the Late Anglo-Saxon Period,* is this the correct question? Equally one needs to ask was the Norman army at Hastings typical? And did the Norman's common experience of warfare, particularly in respect to castle and sieges impact on their use of archery, particularly in comparison to Anglo-Saxon England where, with its more battle centric view of warfare, archers were fragile and thus potentially peripheral.

With the exception of the javelin, missile weapons have always posed an ideological problem for the West's aristocratic military elites. Kipling elucidates the problem brilliantly in his poem *Arithmetic on the Frontier:*

A scrimmage in a Border Station –
A canter down some dark defile –
Two thousand pounds of education
Drops to a ten-rupee jezail –
The Crammer's boast, the Squadron's pride,
Shot like a rabbit in a ride!

Like the French at Agincourt, the Anglo-Saxon elite were trained from an early age to win honour and glory in close-combat with their social equals. Death at a distance threatened to rob them of life's crowning achievement. Yet the bow's obvious military value cannot, and to some degree was not ignored. Thus the bow in the surviving literature is portrayed as a weapon of war:

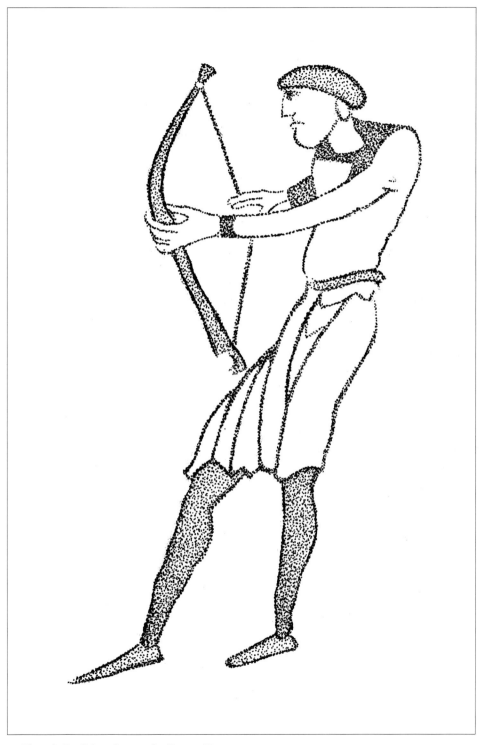

18 The sole English archer on the Bayeux Tapestry.

… he loosed forth many an arrow; sometimes he shot into a shield, sometimes he ripped open a man.

The Battle of Maldon lines 269-70

Also, as a poacher's tool:

… an arrow with a poacher.

Maxims I

Maxims I is also at pains to point out that a soldier uses a shield:

A shield necessarily goes with a soldier.

That the continuation of the 'shield-soldier' (line in *Maxims I*) is 'an arrow with a poacher', appears to emphasise, at least in the eyes of the author of *Maxims I*, the ignoble, (and possibly cowardly) nature of the archer. The image of the archer as ignoble, indeed as evil, is also apparent in *Beowulf*:

The figure of the archer in *Beowulf* is often taken to be a traditional image for the devil and his arrows and as commentators on Hroðgar's speech (*Beowulf* 1700-84) remind us, may allude to St. Paul's injunction to wear spiritual armour against the fiery darts of the evil one (Ephesians vi. 13-18).

Atherton 1993, *The Figure of the Archer in* Beowulf *and the Anglo-Saxon Psalter*

Such attitudes need not, however, prevent the use of the bow in an Anglo-Saxon military context. Pope Urban II in the eleventh century and the Second Lateran Council in the twelfth century both condemned the use of the crossbow amongst Christians. However, this did not prevent its proliferation.

The water is further muddied by the scene on the lid of the Franks Casket (*19*). Here Ægili (Egil), the brother of Weland, is depicted defending his hall with bow and arrow. The fact that not only is the bow an acceptable weapon for a hero, but also that the depiction of archery in a military, as opposed to a hunting context, was deemed a suitable subject for a piece, which displays both learned and aristocratic tastes, further highlights the Anglo-Saxons' apparently ambiguous view of the bow.

Archaeologically (*20* and *21*) although we lack anything comparable to the great continental bog deposits, finds from Bifrons and Chessell Down show that

19 The lid of the Museum Antiquities facsimile of the Franks Casket. *Photograph by Lindsay Allason-Jones.*

the English, unsurprisingly, follow European practice and used the longbow. Of course the problem lies in reconciling the lone English archer in the Bayeux Tapestry with the contradictory literary and scant archaeological evidence.

Norwegian laws of the twelfth and thirteenth century, which were derived from and are believed to reflect earlier Viking practice, required freemen who owed military service to bring a bow, amongst other weapons, when mustered for war. While the appearance of the bow as a weapon of war in Skaldic verse shows that it was not considered entirely contrary to heroism. However, the busy bows at Maldon in 991 did not at all effect the outcome of the battle, and this should caution us against assigning too important a role to Viking archery. As for the bow in later Norwegian laws, such provisions were probably more concerned with the limited naval warfare of the Viking Age, than with the art of war on land in that period. For just as with the English, the Vikings seemed to prefer to settle matters with the heroic ideal of close-order infantry combat, and thus they and most probably for similar reasons placed little reliance on archers. The one obvious archery success story of the period was of course that of the Norman bowmen at Hastings. Yet in this most famous of cases we are looking at something rather atypical.

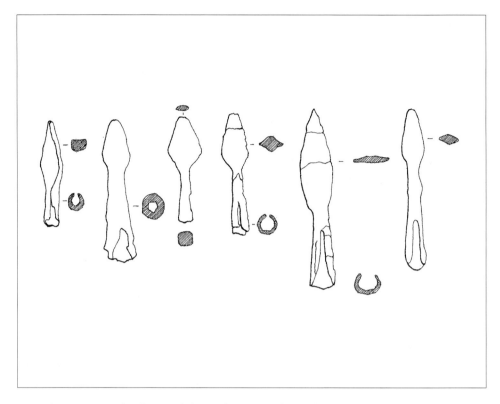

20 Anglo-Saxon arrowheads. From left to right they are from Chalton, Maxey, Durham, Rhuddlan, Empingham, and Thetford. *Redrawn by M. Daniels from Manley 1985.*

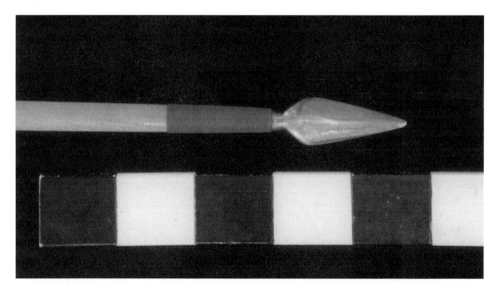

21 A reconstruction of a typical Anglo-Saxon anti-personnel arrowhead.

William's expedition to England and Cortes' to the Yucatan are parallels. Both staked all on success, and in order to help secure the desired outcome they recruited as many followers/mercenaries/adventurers to their cause as possible. Thus although it is impossible to put accurate figures on the number of bowmen (long- and crossbowmen) present in the Duke's army, it is fair to say that the lure of the wealth of one of the richest kingdoms in Europe allowed William to exploit men's greed, and as a consequence field a larger force of archers than was normal for a man in his position. As to where all these archers came from — that is explained by the different tactical situation present on the continent as opposed to Anglo-Saxon England. Or in a word: castles.

Castles were primarily secure bases, designed and located in order to allow armoured, mounted forces to control areas of land. In the attack and defence of such fortifications archers played a vital role. Conversely, in lands where siege warfare was at best peripheral, then the role, presence and numbers of archers may have equally been reduced. Also, at Hastings we remember that the battle lasted all day and that the issue was decided as much by the archers attrition as by the death of Harold II. What of the Welsh? Davies in his 2004 study *Welsh Military Institutions 633-1283*, does not consider the bow to be a weapon of war in Wales until the Anglo-Norman Period. Prior to this point in time it appears to have been used solely in the hunt.

Where then does all of this leave English military archery in the late Anglo-Saxon period?

The *Anglo-Saxon Chronicle* C manuscript's entry for 1066 reference to an archer at the Battle of Stamford Bridge, coupled with the figure of the English archer on the Bayeux Tapestry, have in all probability combined with what we know of the future and led us to ask the wrong questions and to look in the wrong direction.

Whilst there is an undoubted thread of military archery running through the whole of the Anglo-Saxon period, it appears that, at least in England, or rather Britain, the bows contribution to the warfare of the day was rather limited particularly when contrasted with its later successes. The arrow-storms of Agincourt, Towton, Crecy, etc. etc. have cast a long shadow. Equally, the success of the Norman archers at Hastings, coupled with the knowledge that Harold II deployed archers at Stamford Bridge has led to the question — why were they not present, or not present in great numbers, at Hastings? The usual answer that they were the poorest members of the *fyrd*, lacked horses and could not move as rapidly and where thus left behind on the march south — not only smacks of convenience, but also rather ignores their rapid march north. A more probable answer to the question — did the English archers who fought at Stamford Bridge also fight at Hastings? — is *yes*. In the former battle only a small number of archers fought on both sides, while in the latter battle the small contingent of English archers were outnumbered by their opposite numbers on the other side.

Why? Part of the question lies in the Anglo-Viking heroic tradition, and part lies in the Hellenistic Period and the armies of the successor states.

The bow is not and was not a heroic weapon, a useful weapon certainly, but heroic – not really. Even in Homer's vision of the late Mycenaean world the skill of Paris is not regarded as highly as Hector and Achilles' ability to deal out death at close-quarters, and while most people's memory of the end of the *Odyssey* is of Odysseus stringing his great bow, the slaughter of the suitors really gets under way when he dons helmet and takes up shield and spear. Indeed the end of the *Odyssey* provides an object lesson in heroic archery – the well trained warrior should know how to use a bow, and the bow certainly had a use in certain stages, particularly the opening stages, of battle, but a true result the real killing was done up close with spear and sword.

Despite all the sophistication of the Hellenistic warfare, missile troops played a small part in the battles of the day. The reason is simple and it applies equally to the Anglo-Saxon Period and accounts, and explains in large part for the English's ambivalence towards, and decision not to raise or field, large numbers of archers. For to put it quite simply archers were a fragile element in the battle line. From all the evidence it appears that the shield was a more than adequate defence against the archery of the day, and given that, archers were unable to withstand a determined assault by both infantry and cavalry. As a consequence they were confined to the periphery and the main killing was done by the other arms.

CHAPTER FOUR

MILITARY EQUIPMENT, *HERIOTS*, AND THE COMPLETE WARRIOR

There many men lay slain by spears, and northern warriors shot down despite their shields, and Scotsmen too.

Battle of Brunanburh, lines 17-19

Military equipment studies are primarily artefact driven, and here we hit the first problem, for the wealth of the Late Anglo-Saxon period is literary and representational. Of course nothing is perfect, for the Early Anglo-Saxon period is artefact rich, yet literary and representational poor, and really all three are needed to build a complete picture. This lack of archaeology, in the period under study, brings us to our second problem, namely what exactly did the '60 helmets and 60 coats of mail' that Ælfric, Archbishop of Canterbury (1002-5) left to the king in his will look like? Equally when we look at depictions of warriors and scenes in for example Manuscripts *Cotton Cleopatra C VIII, Cotton Claudius B IV,* and *Harley 603*, we need to ask what exactly are we looking at. How accurate are they, not only in terms of the equipment that they depict, but also with respect to the relative frequency of the artefacts shown. Particularly in the latter case with respect to body armour and helmets, for from a brief survey of the manuscripts listed above, body armour, specifically mail, appears to have been far more common than helmets.

Two final factors that must also needs be considered when studying Late Anglo-Saxon military equipment, are the questions of continuity and external influence. The continuity question is straightforward and is basically this – did the equipment styles of the Early Anglo-Saxon period continue into the Late Anglo-Saxon period? The if not, why not question drives us into the realm of external influences, and ultimately leads us to the Bayeux Tapestry with its depiction of the last English army and the question of the antecedents of conical helmets, kite shields and a European wide military fashion.

As well as looking at the form and style of the equipment used, this chapter will also consider what constituted the full panoply of a Late Anglo-Saxon warrior and in the process of reaching this end we must consider the *heriot* or *here-geatu*. *Heriots* being the death-duty of war gear which the law required all those of thegnly rank or above pay, on their passing, to their lord. What exactly was demanded and how we interpret it, helps us to not only build a picture of the complete warrior, but also of a complete army.

ARMOUR

According to *Maxims I* '… to the bold [belongs] a helmet …', while *Maxims II* states that '… blade must strive with helmet in battle …', in *Beowulf* and the *Fight at Finnsburg* the armoured warrior is a recurring leitmotif. Yet in the *Battle of Maldon* armour is mentioned at most once and even this is debatable. Armour also appears on the Franks Casket, the Repton Stone, a fragment of a frieze from Winchester, in manuscript illustrations, and of course on the Bayeux Tapestry. As to the archaeology, well we have four helmets and one set of mail, from England, for the whole of the Anglo-Saxon period. However, to put the archaeology (and possibly the whole question of armour provision in Anglo-Saxon England) in context we must consider the size of the Imperial Roman Army in the mid-second century AD. There is of course no definite answer to the question of how big was the Roman army, we are often dealing with commentators estimates based upon the available evidence. Thus Brian Dobson has arrived at 384,000 (157,000 legionaries and 227,000 auxilia), while Anthony Birley has argued for 415-445,000 men (in the mid-160s AD). Even if we take the lower figure, and bearing in mind the unarmoured slingers and Numidian cavalry depicted on Trajan's Column, we are still looking at well over 300,000 armoured infantry and cavalry. Today, if we brought together every single surviving Roman helmet, not just for the second century AD, but from the period of the Punic Wars to the Islamic Conquest, we would be very lucky to have enough helmets to outfit a single legion (approximately 5000 men). In this light the lack of Anglo-Saxon armour in the archaeological record is put more into perspective.

As to the types of armour used by the English, we must needs in the main consider helmets, shields and body armour. Other armour, specifically greaves and vambraces may also have been used, however, the evidence for their use is circumstantial in the extreme.

HELMETS

With only four extant finds, all of which pre-date the period under study, is it possible to speak of an English or Anglo-Saxon style or type? The answer quite simply is *yes*. The four helmets; Sutton Hoo, Coppergate, Benty Grange and Pioneer, break down into two types (*22* and *colour plate 10*). The first type, which can be described as Romano-Swedish, contains but one example, the helmet from mound 1 at Sutton Hoo. The second type, the English or Anglo-Saxon type, contains the remaining three helmets, which although individually different are enough alike in basics to show a family connection.

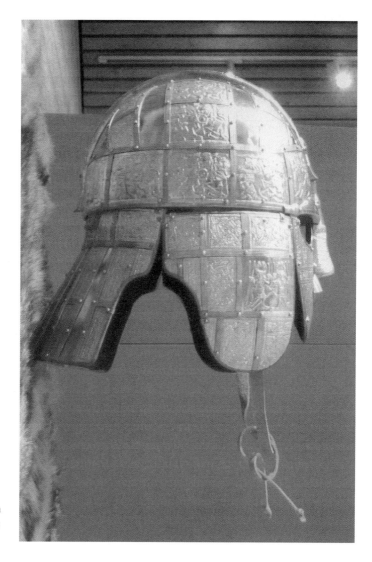

22 A facsimile of the helmet from mound 1, in the museum at Sutton Hoo. *Photograph by Susan Stephenson.*

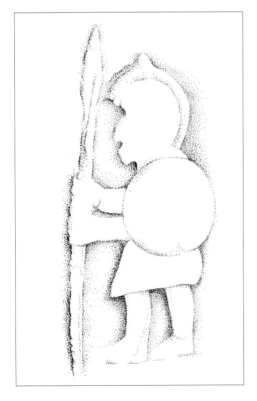

Above: 23 The Brompton warrior. Of note is crested Vendel/Romano-Swedish style helmet he wears.

Right: 24 The Sockburn warrior, as with the Brompton warrior he appears to be wearing a Vendel style helmet.

The helmet from mound 1 at Sutton Hoo has features in common with both late Roman ridge helmets, and the helmet finds from Vendel and Valsgärde in Sweden. Although this is hardly surprising given the fact that the Swedish finds were undoubtedly influenced in their design by late Roman military fashion. Compare for example the Deurne helmet with the Sutton Hoo, Valsgärde 8 and Vendel XIV. Nor should we view the Sutton Hoo helmet as a unique find for this country, for potentially similar Romano-Swedish or Vendel style crested helmets appear on Viking Age sculptures from Sockburn and Brompton (*23* and *24*).

The remaining three helmets – Pioneer, Benty Grange and Coppergate (attempts to rename this last one the 'York' helmet should not be given any credence) – are superficially different; however, they do share a number of features which mark them out as having been designed and constructed along similar lines. In all three cases the helmet's basic structure comprises of a brow band, a crest band and a lateral band. Plates were used to fill the gaps between the bands. Equally in all cases the crest band was extended to form a nasal, while the broad brow band was cut away or open at the front to form eyeholes. Artistically similar helmets appear, in an Anglian context, on the Franks Casket and the Aberlemno Stone.

There exists, to date, only a single practically complete Viking helmet find. Specifically a helmet from a Scandinavian context which is later than the Vendel Period and yet which pre-dates the tenth-century military equipment revolution (if revolution is quite the right word for the changes which will be discussed below). The find in question is the late ninth- or early tenth-century Gjermundbu helmet (*25*). Gjermundbu, certainly when compared to the finds from the Vendel and Valsgärde boat graves, was a very plain and simple object. The helmet consisted of a simple round iron cap, with narrow crest and lateral bands, and a small spike at the apex. The brow band was relatively broad, the eyes and nose of the wearer were protected with spectacles, while mail guarded the neck. Given the level of settlement and trade that took place during and as a result of the First Viking Age it is highly likely that Gjermundbu type helmets were imported into and used, not only in the Danelaw, but throughout the whole of Anglo-Saxon England.

It thus appears that prior to the Second Viking Age a range of helmet types were both available and used in England. Yet for all this wealth of variety (and the use of spangenhelm and lamellar helmets alongside the helmet types discussed above, is also a distinct possibility) it appears that such styles as were popular and common prior to the tenth century, did not survive into the late Anglo-Saxon period. For in the tenth century we see a military equipment revolution. However, having said that this tenth century revolution is probably best compared to the Imperial Roman Army's Antonine equipment revolution of the second century AD – in that it was a change in fashion and form rather than a change in function.

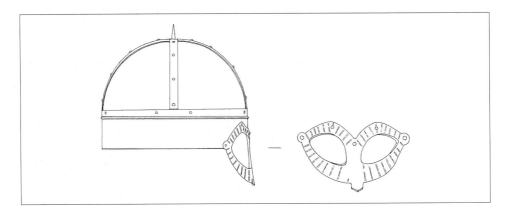

25 The Gjermundbu helmet. *Redrawn by M. Daniels from Grieg 1947.*

The new helmet style which swept Western Europe in the tenth century was not really that new, rather it was the latest version of that old classic – the conical helmet. Conical helmets appear in Assyrian art, on Parthian coins and in use by the Imperial Roman Army. Why this style has proved popular is best explained by examining the variants, both ancient and modern, of this design. Modern examples of the conical helmet are the 'Mitre' cap, the shako, the busby and the bearskin. While it remains true that all of the examples given above, be it Napoleonic shako or Assyrian helmet, provided a crumple zone, this extra protective feature was merely a by-product of the headgear's display function. For all tall headgear was designed to impress, intimidate, and overawe an opponent by the simple expedient of increasing the wearer's height.

As to the specifics of the new helmets themselves, the archaeological evidence from east-central Europe ties in remarkably well with the representational evidence from this country. The Eastern European evidence (*26*, *27*, *28* and *29*), which is itself merely a reflection of contemporary steppe fashion, is an example of hinterland *élan* in the Medieval world. Thus finds of simple helmets, formed from a single piece of iron without a nasal (such as the Hradsko, Bohemia, find) or with an integral nasal (e.g. the Olmütz, Moravia, find) or with a separate, attached nasal (e.g. the St. Wenceslas helmet, in Prague) appear on the Bayeux Tapestry, and in British Library manuscripts *Cotton Cleopatra C VIII*, *Cotton Claudius B IV*, *Harley 603*, and on a coin (dated 1053-6) of Edward the Confessor. Segmented helmets – such as a poorly provenanced example in the Metropolitan museum of Art, New York, and a gilded Polish helmet, currently on loan to the Royal Armouries from Liverpool Museum – appear on the head of Goliath in the British Library *Ms. Cotton Tiberius C VI*, and of course on the Bayeux Tapestry. Conical helmets also appear on tenth-century Viking sculpture from Middleton and Sockburn (*30*, *31* and *32*).

26 A reconstruction of the tenth-century Hradsko helmet.

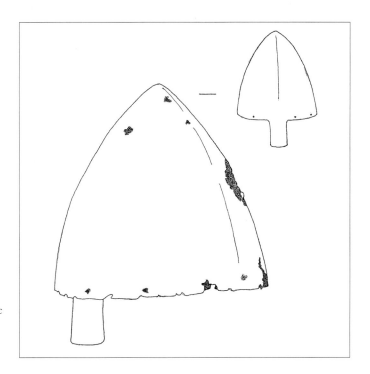

27 The eleventh-century Olmutz helmet, the classic 'Norman' style helmet. *Redrawn by M. Daniels from Nicolle 1988.*

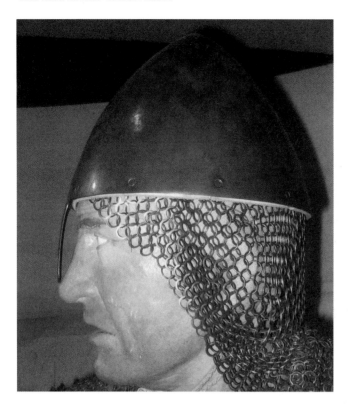

Left: 28 A reconstruction of the Olmutz helmet, on the head of a Norman. In the Yorkshire Museum, York.

Below: 29 The St Wenceslaus helmet, including a detail of the nasal. *Redrawn by M. Daniels from Nicolle 1988.*

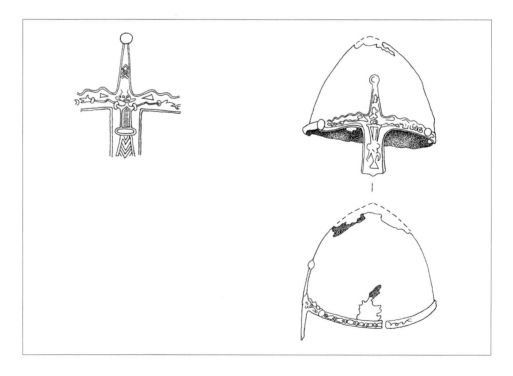

Cheek pieces, on conical helmets, which are known from the twelfth-century Lewis chessmen, do not appear to have been used in this period. Some of the helmets on the Bayeux Tapestry appear to have an extension on the back of the helmet. This may represent a neck guard, equally, illustrations of conical helmets which both pre- and post-date the Tapestry show such helmets with decorative and/or identification (the purpose is uncertain) ribbons hanging from the back of the helmets in much the same place as these extensions. Thus the Bayeux Tapestry may be showing us ribbons rather than neck guards. Where protection for the neck and the side of the face is shown (although none survives archaeologically from this period) it takes the form of either a mail coif, or a mail hood which is integral with the body of the hauberk.

Before going on to consider the question of the level of helmet ownership an aspect of the representational evidence needs to be considered. For with manuscript depictions of headgear we are at times defeated by the simplicity of the illustrations. Thus we need to ask, is what is being shown a hat, a helmet, or a helmet covered by some form of decorative covering?

The mounted army depicted in the eleventh-century British Library *Ms. Cotton Claudius B IV (33)* in many ways typifies the problem as a whole – what do the various cone-shaped pieces of headgear worn by the riders represent? It is of course entirely possible that they simply represent hats made from either cloth or leather. Leather helmets we will, however, dismiss as a fiction without evidence. Decorative helmet covers, although a feature of the Byzantine and Islamic worlds, do not appear to have been a feature of north-west European warfare and can thus be discounted. The final possibility is that all of the warriors are helmeted, and this is not as far fetched a possibility as it may seem. The straight cones in the manuscript illustration represent simple conical helmets. Unequivocal depictions of conical helmets with forward-pointing peaks are known from both contemporaneous and earlier Carolingian manuscripts, and these may also be shown, and provide an explanation for the cone headgear with forward pointing peaks in *Ms. Cotton Claudius B IV* and other late Anglo-Saxon manuscripts. Finally, the rumpled cone shapes. Although usually interpreted as folds of cloth, they could equally represent fluted helmets. Generally viewed as a later Western style, flute helmets are known from both Carolingian and post-Carolingian illustrations and certainly existed in the Islamic world by the eleventh century at the latest.

How common were helmets?

1008. Here the king [Aethelred] ordered that they should determinedly build ships all over England: that is, one warship from three hundred and 10 hides, and from 8 hides a helmet and mailcoat.

Anglo-Saxon Chronicle E manuscript

30 One of three (see also figures *31* and *32*) tenth-century conical helmeted warriors from Middleton. It is also worth noting that the three warriors were all appear to have been, when originally carved, surrounded by their complete panoply of shield, spear, sword, axe and seax.

31 The tenth-century head of warrior from Middleton.

32 A tenth-century warrior cross fragment from Middleton.

Brooks argues that the *Anglo-Saxon Chronicle* entry for 1008 saw the English finally become comparable, in equipment terms, with their continental counterparts. Certainly the chronicle entry, combined with the *heriots* and the surviving wills of the same period, seems to point to a great deal of armour (the provision or otherwise of body armour prior to 1008 is discussed later in this chapter). Universality is, however, another matter. The representational and literary sources, supported by the evidence of *heriots*, points to different levels of provision dependant upon status, and indeed this conclusion is borne out by comparison with Carolingian capitularies.

In answer to the question – how common were helmets? – the answer is probably that helmets were far more common than body armour. Indeed, if one considers armour provision and the history of close-order infantry combat from its beginnings in ancient Greece up to the AD 1066 (leaving to one side the armour high point of the Imperial Roman Army in the first and second centuries AD) then the general pattern was for the provision of at least a helmet and a shield, with a part of the army having helmet, shield and body armour. It is to this minimum standard (helmet and shield, with some helmet, shield and body armour) that all English armies aspired. It may well be that the wealth of the late Anglo-Saxon State allowed this standard to be exceeded, with a greater proportion of body armoured men to non-body armoured men, and this may well explain the *Anglo-Saxon Chronicle*, E ms., entry for 1008 and its supporting evidence.

33 Helmets or hats? Details of heads of warriors from the eleventh-century British Library Ms. Cotton Claudius B IV.

SHIELDS

The shield in the late Anglo-Saxon Period shows evidence of both continuity and change. Continuity in that the large, circular flat shield of the early Anglo-Saxon Period continued in use until the Battle of Hastings. Change in that by 1066 it had mostly been replaced by the kite shield.

The Early Anglo-Saxon shield, the shield of the Migration Period and the First Viking Wars continued remarkably unchanged into the late Anglo-Saxon Period. Indeed why should it not? The design itself had remained unchanged from at least the third century AD, if not earlier (for a more detailed description and discussion of the Anglo-Saxon shield see Stephenson, I.P., *The Anglo-Saxon Shield*). In basic terms the shield consisted of a large (diameter 84-118cm) circular, flat or slightly convex (in one plane only) wooden board. Although the Viking-period Gokstad finds show that the board need not be covered, generally a leather covering on either the front, or the rear, or on both sides of the shield board was employed. The shield was edged with either a metal or leather rim, which was sewn in place. The shield was held by a single central grip, the hand being protected by a metal shield boss, and it is in this metal shield boss that we potentially see the only real break with the past (*34, 35* and *36*).

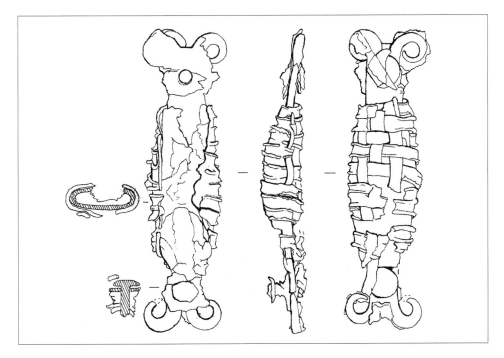

34 The shield grip from grave 126, Morning Thorpe Anglo-Saxon Cemetery, Norfolk. *Redrawn by M. Daniels from Green, Rogerson and White 1987.*

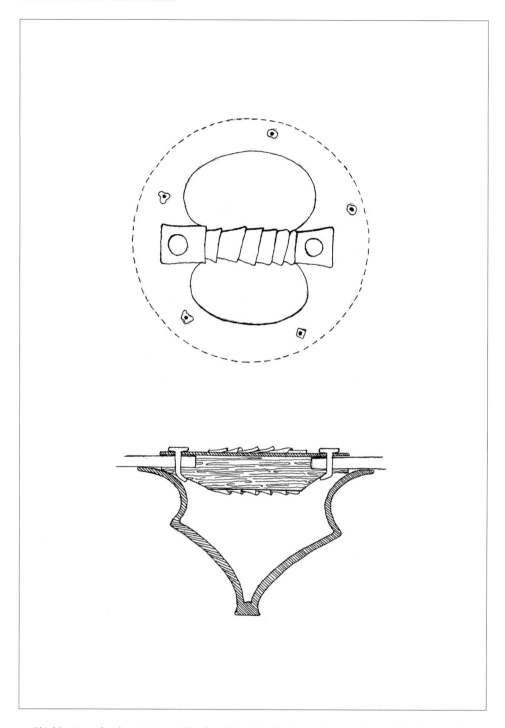

35 Shield grip technology. It is possible that this style of grip attachment, along with the type of grip illustrated in figure 34 continued in use and was used on the round shields carried by some of the English on the Bayeux Tapestry. *Redrawn by M. Daniels from Brown 1980.*

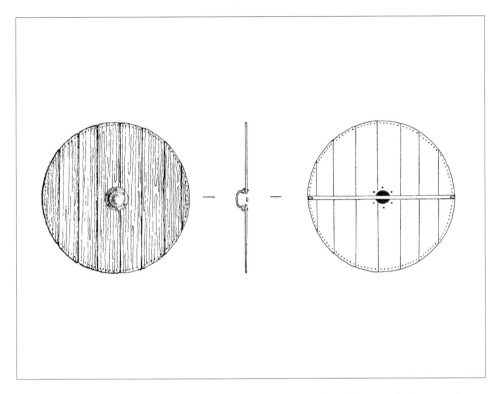

36 A shield from the Viking Period Gokstad ship. This type of shield with its simple, long wooden grip could represent the circular style carried by the English at Hastings. *Redrawn by M. Daniels from Nicolaysen 1882.*

As with helmets, we are left in a position where we have to interpret representational evidence in the light of earlier finds and contemporaneous parallels. For from the evidence of the surviving manuscript illustrations it appears that the earlier styles of shield boss were replaced by a new conical form. It is of course entirely possible that the lack of continuity is more imagined than real, and that scribal simplicity, in the case of a minor artefact such as the shield boss, has glossed over the continued use of the Sugar-Loaf shield boss (Evison types e and f) into the late Anglo-Saxon period (*37, 38* and *39*). Equally, conical and sub-conical forms are known from tenth-and eleventh-century Byzantine and Scandinavian contexts. Given the ease of transmission of military equipment forms from east to west (see above – helmets, and below – kite shields) it seems likely that even if Sugar-Loaf bosses continued in use, that they co-existed alongside other non-native conical forms. It is also likely that the more common, archaeologically at least, Viking domed shield boss (see for example the finds from the Gokstad ship) were adopted by the English in the First Viking Age and continued in use into the Second (*40*).

37 Goliath as an eleventh-century Anglo-Saxon Warrior. From British Library *Ms. Cotton Tiberius C VI.*

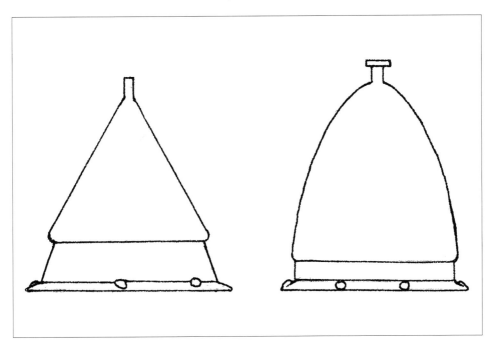

38 Sugar-Loaf shield bosses. Evison types E (left) and F (right). *Redrawn by M. Daniels from Evison 1963.*

39 A Sugar-Loaf shield boss in the Ashmolean Museum, Oxford. It is possible, but by no means certain, that this type of shield boss continued into the late Anglo-Saxon period.

40 A typical Viking period shield boss in the British Museum.

The kite, or as it is sometimes erroneously called the 'Norman' shield (for as will be seen the Normans did not invent it, although it must be said that they are most associated with it in this country), is yet another example, if one were needed, of the fact that Anglo-Saxon England, indeed Western Europe as a whole, was not some isolated military pocket, rather that it was connected to and influenced by the peoples of the steppes, the Islamic world, and Byzantium. The adoption of the kite shield in the eleventh century (and for that matter the conical helmet in the tenth) shows that the English were part of the mainstream of European military culture (*41* and *42*).

The dominance of the kite shield, over other forms, is demonstrated by its ubiquity on the Bayeux Tapestry. The reasons behind its rise are, as will be seen, also understandable, its origins are, however, harder to ascertain. The kite shield appeared first in the Byzantine and Islamic worlds, although given our current state of knowledge, it is impossible to state either where it was first developed, or if we are looking at a case of simultaneous development. The Byzantine *Sylloge tacticorum* (38.1), which dates to *c.*AD 950, describes Byzantine infantry shields which were broad at the top and narrow at the bottom – kite shaped in fact. Even here though the Byzantines may not have been the originators of the design, in that it may have been adapted from an Iranian infantry shield. Alternatively, it may have first appeared in Umayyad Andalus. A fragment of painted stucco found in the ruins of the Moorish palace at Madina-al-Zahra near Cordoba in Spain and dated to the tenth century, shows an armoured cavalryman with a large kite shield.

If the origins of the kite shield are obscure then the same cannot be said for the reasons behind the rapidity of its adoption beyond its first home, nor its continued popularity. It continued in this, its early form, until *c.*1150-1200, from this date on it became more triangular in shape and this large triangular shield continued to be used until *c.*1250, at which point we see more evolution.

No extant examples survive from this period, however it is possible to attempt, based upon the representational evidence and later surviving examples, a reconstruction. In the course of which the reasons behind the popularity of the shield will become apparent.

Kite shields, in this period, appear to have been approximately 60cm wide at their widest point and 120cm long. They were in all probability constructed from planks and covered with leather. In terms of thickness, a late twelfth-century example in the Swiss National Museum in Zurich was made from wood 15mm thick. The Swiss example was covered in parchment, which may also have been used in the period under discussion, despite II Æthelstan 15 and III Æthelstan 8. Certainly in terms of thickness this is greater than earlier Anglo-Saxon shields, which by the seventh century only averaged 8.5mm. Indeed it is also thicker than Imperial Roman plank shields, which show thickness' similar to the early English examples. Kite shields were either flat (they are shown being used as a table on the Bayeux Tapestry), or slightly convex in the horizontal plane (as is shown in the *c.*1140-50 'Temple Pyx'). Anything other than slightly convex can be discounted as this would make them unusable on horseback. Rims are definitely apparent from the representational evidence, and were probably most commonly made of leather (possibly *cuir bouilli* or rawhide), although metal rims cannot be discounted. The rim was probably held in place by sewing or in the case of a metal rim, sewing and clips.

41 A reconstruction of kite shield in the Yorkshire Museum, York.

42 Facsimiles of eleventh-century southern Italian or Sicilian ivory chessmen. Along with the body-armour and conical helmet, it is worth noting the size and coverage afforded by the figures' kite shields.

Despite depictions of shield bosses on kite shields on the Bayeux Tapestry, the shield was not held solely in one hand. The bosses shown on the Bayeux Tapestry and on other depictions of the kite shield were decorative, although they may have served a limited offensive function. Equally, those shields on the Bayeux Tapestry which appear to have simply a single strap on the rear of the shield, should be ignored as a simplification of the true picture. Rather the shield was held (on the left arm) using a series of leather straps (brases or enarmes) which formed a combined arm and handgrip (similar in concept to the grip arrangement on the Greek *hoplon*). The forearm rested against an oblong pad. A shoulder or neck strap (a guige) was also fitted, this strap was probably adjustable (with a buckle) (*43*).

The kite shield, when compared to its predecessor the circular shield, was a large shield – it was longer, thicker and heavier, yet we should not see it as unwieldy. Nor should we view it as better, rather we should view it in its context. For a horse riding warrior aristocracy who were expected to be able to fight on both foot and horse (and possibly more on horseback than was previously the norm) and certainly from a continental viewpoint with the riser of the crossbow, it was ideally suited to the tactical circumstances of the day. On horseback it protected the whole of the riders left side, on foot in the shield wall it offered protection to the vulnerable lower left leg. The increased thickness and thus weight was compensated for by the new carrying mechanism and was designed to give the defence an edge over the attack.

43a and 43b Various methods of kite shield grip and suspension, as illustrated on the Bayeux Tapestry.

BODY ARMOUR

> Then an armed man approached the earl; he wanted to acquire that warrior's armrings, reaf and gold bands, and the ornamented sword.

> *The Battle of Maldon*, lines 159-61

Reaf means, according Clark Hall's *A Concise Anglo-Saxon Dictionary*, 'plunder, booty, spoil, garment, armour, vestment.' Scragg in his *The Battle of Maldon*, translates it as robe (or garment), others, but by no means all, have preferred the armour meaning of the word. How this word has been understood, for it is the only possible mention of the use of armour by the English in the whole poem, has affected peoples understanding of the warfare of the period.

Halsall, while accepting that metal helmets and armour could have been easily produced in the Early Medieval West, argues that from the 950s English armies engaged in mobile warfare against the Welsh and the Scots, may have discarded their armour. Brooks, arguing that the English at Maldon in AD 991 were unarmoured, sees them as inadequately equipped, unable to fight at close quarters and reluctant and unable to stand against an enemy superior in terms of equipment.

In the summer of 168 BC, at Pydna, Greece, in a short, hard fought, bloody fight at close quarters, the armoured might of Rome crushed Macedon. According to Polybius (XXIX.17):

> Aemilius the consul, who had never seen a phalanx until this occasion in the war with Perseus, often confessed afterwards to certain persons in Rome that he had never seen anything more terrible and dreadful than a Macedonian phalanx, and this although he had witnessed and directed as many battles as any man.

And the most terrible part of that dreadful army? According to Plutarch it was the Theban contingent, who were armoured solely with shield and greaves. During the principate of Domitian, at Mons Graupius in Scotland, armoured Imperial Roman auxiliary infantry attacked uphill, slaughtering their barbarian opponents (Tacitus, *Agricola*, 36). Armour was not a bar to movement, nor did it prevent the wearer fighting in raiding and skirmish warfare, the Anglo-Scottish Border Reivers it must be remembered were armoured, neither did the lack of it prevent close-order infantry combat. Nor (see below, chapter 5) was its presence (or absence for that matter) the reason for the English defeat at Maldon.

The armoured warrior was an Anglo-Saxon leitmotif, he appears in *Beowulf*, *The Fight at Finnsburg*, in *Judith*, in *Andreas* and in *Elene*, on the Franks Casket, the Repton Stone, on a fragment of a frieze from Winchester, in numerous manuscript illustrations and of course on the Bayeux Tapestry. Body armour formed a part of the artistic milieu of the aristocracy, equally it formed a very real part of their material culture. For English armies were a part of the mainstream of European military culture (witness the swift adoption of conical helmets and kite shields) and thus little different from their European counterparts, and they were generally well armoured. There is no real reason, nor evidence to support the hypothesis that armour was either absent from, or temporarily abandoned by, English armies in the late Anglo-Saxon period. Thus at Maldon, or rather in the poem, *reaf* is probably best translated as armour, indeed given Byrhtnoth's position and status it is highly unlikely that he went to battle unarmoured (*44, 45, 46, 47, 48, 49* and *50*).

44 Mail armoured 'Warriors in procession' from the Valsgärde 7 helmet.

Above: 45 Mail clad and helmeted
warriors. A detail from the lid of
the Franks Casket.

Right: 46 Eleventh-century English
warriors wearing short mail shirts
and conical helmets. From British
Library *Ms. Cotton Cleopatra C VIII.*

47 An eleventh-century king wearing knee-length mail, with elbow-length sleeves. The slit at the front is to allow the armour to be worn even if the wearer is mounted. From British Library *Ms. Cotton Claudius B IV*.

How then should we view the *Anglo-Saxon Chronicle's*, E manuscript, entry for 1008, and the appearance at around the same time of armour in *heriots*? Certainly not as a sudden rush too introduce armour in order to achieve parity with an enemy superior in equipment. Rather we should see it as an attempt to bring the nation's wealth into play in order to increase and formalise the provision of an existing resource. For the protective effect of armour is both individual and cumulative. A line (or lines) of armoured men, in close-order, have a tactical advantage over a similar unarmoured formation, in that they are harder to kill. The Romans had the resources to equip whole units, indeed whole armies, with metal body armour. The late Anglo-Saxon State, although doubtless aware of the cumulative value of armour, was not able to do as much as Imperial Rome. It was, however, probably the most centralised, organised state in Europe at that time, with a competent revenue raising system and an efficient administration. Thus we should see the late Anglo-Saxon State attempting to provide, if not necessarily whole armies of armoured warriors, at least ranks of them.

48 An armoured representation of
Goliath, from British Library *Ms. Harley
603.*

49 English art, like the literature of the
Anglo-Saxon period, is not lacking in
representations of armoured figures. The
short mail shirt in this illustration is from
the British Library *Ms Cotton Cleopatra
C VIII.*

50 An armoured English thegn from the Bayeux Tapestry.

The predominant form of body armour was mail, and it appears to have come in a variety of styles: waist length, with short sleeves (British Library *Ms. Cotton Cleopatra C VIII*), knee length, split front and back, with short or elbow length sleeves (British Library *Ms. Cotton Claudius B IV*), knee length, split front and back, with ¾ length sleeves (British Library *Ms. Harley 603*), knee length – this is what the apparent shorts most probably represent – split front and back, with ¾ length sleeves, integral hood and ventail (The Bayeux Tapestry).

The edged square seen on some mail shirts on the Bayeux Tapestry is probably best interpreted as a ventail (an integral flap of mail designed to protect the mouth and lower face, which was tied in place (*51*)), as a re-enforcing square of mail on the chest would not require the leather edging it is depicted as having, whereas a ventail would. Indeed it also appears that as well as edging the ventail, the leather (the leather is supposition, but it is a likely supposition) also held in place a lining, such as the one shown in the *Hrabanus Maurus* manuscript at Monte Cassino. Mail which had a slight hole to allow the sword hilt to pass through, and where the body of the sword was worn and suspended beneath the armour appears, from the Bayeux Tapestry, to have been more of a Norman and not English fashion; although, the style would not have been unknown in this country.

Archaeologically the seventh-century mail shirt from mound 1 at Sutton Hoo seems to have been long sleeved and knee length, while the fourth- or fifth-century Vimose and the eighth- to eleventh-century Vaerdalen, North Trondelag and Romel, Melhus, South Trondelag (although not completely intact) appear to have been at least hip length with elbow length sleeves. The mail from the Gjermundbu find is, sadly, fragmentary. In all save one case, prior to the adoption of the hooded ventail form, all the evidence (representational and particularly the archaeological) points to a simple wide-necked cuirass. The exception being two figures engaged in combat portrayed in the British Library *Ms. Cotton Cleopatra C VIII*. Here the two warriors, who are both wearing short sleeved waist length mail, have very tight neck closure which appears to have been facilitated by a short closed slit at the front of the neck. How this worked in practice (if it is not scribal error) is unknown – there is no evidence for the hooks or breastplates the Roman Period for example – but its existence is not outside the bounds of possibility.

Besides mail, the possibility exists that lamellar was also worn. Finds from the Viking site of Birka, in Sweden, have been dated to AD 900-950. The Birka finds, which appear to be of Old Turkic origin, were probably obtained either via the Rus, or from Byzantium. Lamellar, even in the Roman Period, was never a popular form of armour in the West, yet finds such as those from Birka, from Charavines in Provence, Niederstotzingen, and of course Wisby, along with the Isola Rizza dish and a ninth-century Carolingian ivory in the cathedral treasury in Nancy,

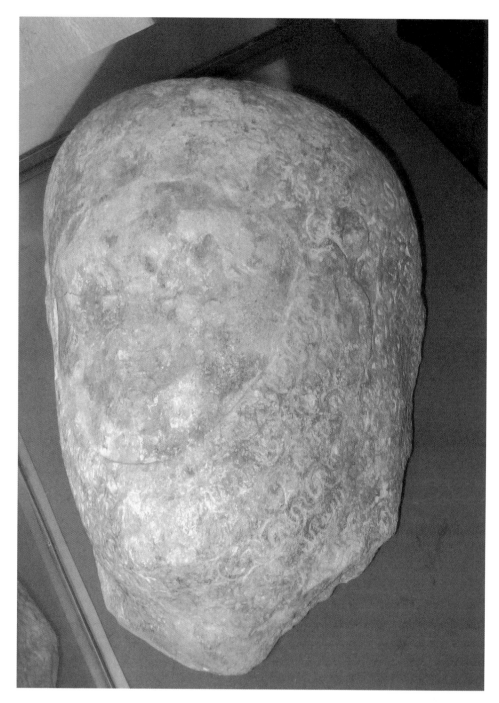

51 A mailed knight's head (possibly thirteenth century) from Reading Abbey, currently in Reading Museum. Of interest is the fact that the ventail follows eleventh-century fashion and is tied on both sides of the head (only the left hand side is visible in this photograph).

show that lamellar was worn in Western Europe, even if only in a limited manner, from the end of the Roman Period through until the fourteenth century. It is thus possible that it was also used, again to a limited extent, in Anglo-Saxon England.

Limb defences, greaves and vambraces, may also have had a limited currency in Late Anglo-Saxon England. We of course have the earlier Valsgärde finds, along with Byzantine evidence and their mention in Carolingian written sources. Whether or not all this adds up to their use by the English is another matter. At best it remains a possibility.

Finally, before turning to the subject of weapons, let us consider under-armour padding. Despite the lack of direct evidence for its use by the English, the fact remains that armour does not work properly without it and it was therefore undoubtedly used. In terms of its actual form we must look to earlier evidence, the Roman *thoracomachus* (see Stephenson, I.P., *Romano-Byzantine Infantry Equipment* for a full discussion of this artefact), and later evidence, the Medieval *gambeson* and *aketon*. The Roman and Medieval versions of under-armour padding were probably very similar in form and thus it is highly likely that the Anglo-Saxon version of the garment was the same as its earlier and later counterparts, namely two layers of linen padded in between with wool and quilted vertically.

WEAPONS

Gormenghast, Peake's great creation was defined, to use his own words, by 'ritual's footprints.' Now this is not to say that where *Gormanghast* was ritual, the Anglo-Saxon's were without ritual. The Anglo-Saxon elite were a Christian, warrior aristocracy – indeed these words define not only themselves but also their view of their religion – for Christ in the *Heliand*, and in other more native English works, is a warleader. For the elite of Anglo-Saxon England, like all such groups, ritual helped define their existence and position in society. In Peake's creation, however, the past had come to control, dominate and stagnate the present.

For the Anglo-Saxon's view of the past, in relation to weapons and warfare, we must first turn to Machiavelli. Today, Machiavelli's most famous work is *The Prince*, his great political treatise on *realpolitik*. During his lifetime, however, it was another matter, for the only major work of his to published (and incidentally widely read and esteemed) while still alive was *The Art of War*. In it, Machiavelli, when commenting on the Swiss notes that:

... all the other nations in Europe have adopted the same weapons and manner of fighting.

Niccolò Machiavelli, 1521, *The Art of War*, bk.2

Successful armies are copied, armaments are imitated. Nor should this be viewed as a new process, the Hellenistic armies of the successor states, which were modelled on Philip's great creation the Macedonian phalanx, were themselves reformed along Roman lines in the 160s BC. The Swiss pike formations were copied to some extent and then employed, albeit with disastrous results, by the Scots at Flodden in 1513. Later we see hussars being copied across Europe, while in the nineteenth century, across the world, pickelhaube replaced képi. In the twentieth century the success of the AK-47 can in part be attributed to the fact that its effectiveness is combined with a simple yet robust design.

Returning to the matter in hand, the question is this – did, as some have argued, the weapon styles of the early Anglo-Saxon period continue in use into the late Anglo-Saxon period? To give an example – did the range of spearheads, as categorised by Swanton, continue to be used by the English at Maldon and Hastings? The short answer – it is possible, but it is rather unlikely. Weapons in the late Anglo-Saxon period were both static and fluid. Static in that we see the same types as in the early and middle Anglo-Saxon periods, fluid in that they adapted to current military fashion.

It holds true of course that merely adopting the latest in military fashion is not always enough, for if we examine for example the Janissaries and the adoption of European firearms, or the Scots at Flodden, we see other processes at work. In the former case European tactics and discipline were not adopted along with European weapons, this adoption of one aspect rather than the whole package helps to explain the Ottoman's defeat at Lepanto. The same holds true for Scots at Flodden, here we see an enthusiastic adoption of only a part of the weapons system (pike and artillery – crucially they failed, due to cost, to invest in halberds, two-handed swords and crossbows) coupled with a lack of training, leading to catastrophic results.

We see nothing, however, quite so dramatic with late Anglo-Saxon military equipment. Even if the events which led to the change in style, namely the First Viking Age and the unification of England were dramatic in themselves, the changes that occurred took place more along what could be called 'Roman' lines. With Roman military equipment weapons conformed to a basic 'fire & shock' pattern on top of a close-order infantry mould. Thus the changes could be categorised as being more of style than of substance. The English were essentially the same, for with one exception – the broad axe – and that as will be seen may well have been a response to a new tactical situation, the weapons of the

Migration Period and the weapons of Hastings differed in aesthetic rather than in practical terms.

The catalyst for the aesthetic changes, the final nails in the coffin of the earlier styles, came from the Viking raiders (later armies and settlers) who first appeared in AD 789. The changes that occurred were not only the inevitable result of a new dynamic cultural input, they were also unsurprising. Unsurprising in that we see changes in style and appearance prior to the First Viking Age and there is thus every reason to believe that change would have occurred and continued to occur even without the Vikings – they merely added to the mix. Inevitable – well we are back to the copying of successful armies. What then were the changes and what did they amount to? We will begin by considering that popular perennial, the sword.

Bone, in his 1989 paper *The Development of Anglo-Saxon Swords from the Fifth to the Eleventh Century*, notes that in general terms English swords varied little, in terms of their overall dimensions, over the period as a whole. These dimensions being, overall length 81-97cm, blade length 68-81cm, and blade width (at the lower guard) 4.5-6.5cm. However, if we look at Geibig's classification of Viking sword blades we see a slightly different picture. For Geibig's Type 5 (blade length 84-91cm, blade width 4.8-5.1cm) which was in use from the mid-tenth through to the mid- to late eleventh century, was slightly longer than Bone's general analysis, while his Type 4 (which was in use at roughly the same time as the Type 5) was a smaller weapon, with a blade length of 63-76cm and a blade width of 4.5-5.0cm. Thus Bone's statement whilst essentially true needs qualifying with respect to Geibig, and as a result we should therefore expect that the English, in the period under study, fought with a greater range of swords (in terms of size) than was previously supposed.

Viking swords, particularly the hilt, have been long and extensively studied. As a result the subject has accrued a respectable corpus. The foundation text is of course Petersen's 1919 *De Norske Vikingesverd*. The main English works on the subject being Wheeler's 1927 catalogue for the Museum of London entitled *London and the Vikings*, Oakeshott's 1960 *The Archaeology of Weapons*, and most recently Peirce's 2002 *Swords of the Viking Age*, all of which build on Petersen's work. It is in the form of the hilt, resultant from Viking influence, that we see the greatest change and the defining break between early and late Anglo-Saxon swords. We thus see pommels and guards wholly of iron (although as the illustrations show, there was the odd exception, in material, if not form, terms), with, over time, pommels and upper guards becoming a single piece (*52, 53, 54* and *55*). In terms of pommel styles, it is to be expected that Viking styles would have occurred alongside indigenous 'tea-cosy' or 'mushroom' style pommels (for a detailed discussion and listing of pommel types the works of Bone and Peirce are probably the best place to start).

Above: 52 Tenth-century English sword hilts. From left to right they are from Witham, Shifford, Mileham, and Battersea. *Redrawn by M. Daniels from Bone 1989.*

Left: 53 The hilt of an eleventh-century sword from the Thames at Battersea, in the Ashmolean Museum.

54 A tenth-century sword from the Thames at Temple, in the British Museum. The hilt is decorated with animal ornament and the grip is bound with silver wire.

55 Showing that not all sword hilts in this period were metal. These fitting in the Yorkshire Museum, York, are from different Viking period swords, the pommel is whalebone, while the guard is plain bone.

Scabbards rarely survive in the archaeological record. For Anglo-Saxon England scabbards, with the exception of fragments adhering to blades, do not survive at all. However, such evidence as we do have, combined with appropriate parallels (from Germanic bog finds and from the Roman world), allows us to accurately reconstruct the structure of the scabbard. Two thin pieces of wood surrounded the blade, although plain wooden examples are known, albeit from the Nydam find, generally the outside of the scabbard was covered with leather or cloth. A greased or oiled internal lining, again of cloth or leather, but also at times of fur, was present in order to protect the sword blade. Such a lining helped to hold the sword firmly in the scabbard, yet it did not impede drawing. Decorative chapes and scabbard mouths appear to have been used throughout the period, see for example the late eleventh-century carving at Ebberston Church near Scarborough. Their use does not, however, appear to have been universal, and they are absent from the Bayeux Tapestry. In all cases the scabbard should be viewed as a thing of beauty, a means by which images of martial terror, and personal wealth, could be projected. Indeed if we consider feudal Japan, it should be noted that while their sword blades are beautiful, their scabbards are exquisite.

Our understanding of sword suspension in this period is problematic to say the least (56, 57 and 58). Cameron, in her work on sheaths and scabbards, appears to have identified indentations, which may have been created by scabbard slides, on a number of leather scabbard covers from York and Gloucester. Following the fall of the Roman Empire in the West, scabbard slides lost their pre-eminent position, thus we also see the use of scabbard bosses or buttons (such as in the case of the sword from mound 1 at Sutton Hoo), and a form of ring suspension from the Viking graves at Ballateare and Cronk Moar. Whether all of these systems continued in use into the late Anglo-Saxon period is hard to ascertain as such evidence as we have is representational and simplistic in the extreme. The Winchester fragment probably shows a crossed leather strap, the Bayeux Tapestry in the main shows a single line which appears to be a part of the sword belt, although on one occasion the tapestry shows two parallel horizontal bands and on another a double buckled sword belt. British Library *Ms. Cotton Tiberius C VI*'s Goliath has a decorated baldric which wraps once around the scabbard. Whether you use a sword belt or a baldric, and both appear to have been used, the fact remains that it must be held securely in place and at present the current state of the evidence does not allow us to say how this was done. Although it is possible that in the surviving art we are seeing the beginnings of the elaborate thonging and lacing, which secured the sword belt to the scabbard in the post-1066 medieval world.

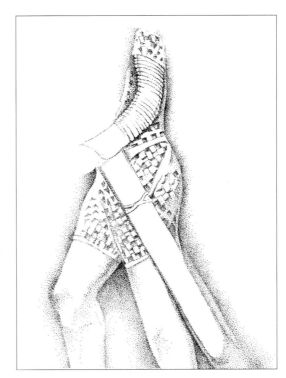

Right: 56 Of note is the sword suspension on the armoured figure on a fragment of a frieze from the Old Minster, Winchester.

Below: 57 Early Anglo-Saxon sword suspension, from mound 1 at Sutton Hoo. *Redrawn by M. Daniels from Bruce-Mitford 1978.*

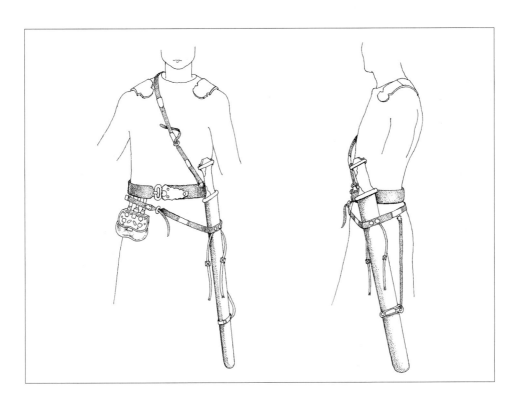

58 Sutton Hoo style sword suspension in the late tenth and eleventh centuries. A detail from Bodleian Library, *Junius II*.

1 Reconstruction 1 – Byrhtnoth at Maldon,
AD 991.

2 Reconstruction 2 – lesser thegn, *c.*AD 1066.

Left: *3* Reconstruction 3 – housecarl, *c.*AD 1066.

Below: *4* Reconstruction 4 – King Harold II,
Godwinson, AD 1066.

5 Corfe Castle in Dorset. The site of the murder of Edward the Martyr.

6 Oxford Cathedral and the site of St Frideswide's minister, where a massacre of Danes took place on St Brice's Day 1002.

7 & 8 Strategic mobility – the Skuldelev 5 warship. Vessels such as this powered the military adventures of Swein and Cnut.

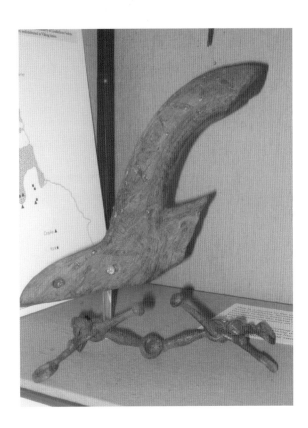

9 A part of a Viking saddle and horse's bit, from York. In the Yorkshire Museum, York.

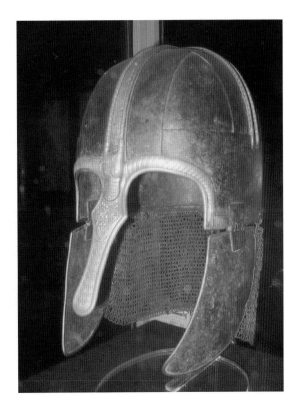

10 The Coppergate Helmet, an Anglo-Saxon type helmet. In the Yorkshire Museum, York.

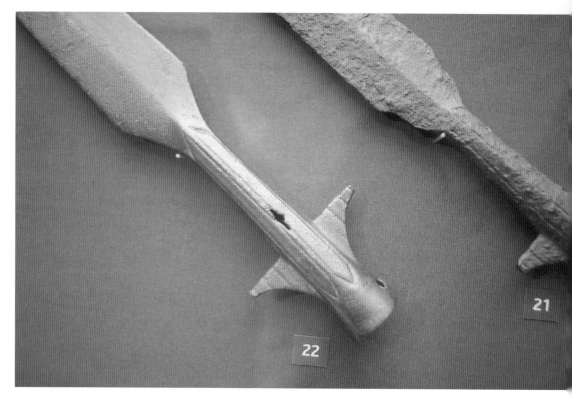

11 A detail of the decoration on a Carolingian type 'winged' spearhead, in the British Museum. In this period the decoration of spears had moved from the shaft to the socket.

12 The east-side of Northey Island, looking towards the mouth of the Blackwater. This part of the island was the site of Viking landing in AD 991.

13 The east-side of Northey Island, this time looking towards Maldon, which is completely shielded from sight by the hill.

14 The causeway, as seen from the island. Of particular note in the foreground is the clinging, impassable mud which forms the bed of the Blackwater.

15 Northey Island from the mainland. Of particular note is the hill which forms the centre of the island.

16 The site of the Battle of Maldon AD 991.

59 The seax from the Thames at Battersea, in the British Museum.

That the seax was carried into battle is not in doubt, whether it was used, or rather whether one form of the object was used in combat, is. Of the two forms of the seax that are known from the late Anglo-Saxon period, one - the long or sword seax - is easily dealt with. English examples (59), although shorter than their Viking counterparts, which had 80-90cm blade lengths, were still between 54-76cm long in terms of blade length and thus perfectly adequate as mêlée weapons. Late Viking single edged swords with Petersen Type X hilts have also been found, and while it is possible that English long seaxes may have been fitted with sword hilts, it is equally possible that they had simple hilts or grips without guard or pommel. The 'shorter', so to speak, long seax would have been suspended horizontally at the waist, as is shown on the Repton Stone, whereas those at the other end of the blade length spectrum would have been worn as a sword on the left hip. It is also probable, as both the Continental evidence and the more native Repton Stone show, the long seax was at times carried alongside, and tertiary to, the spear and the sword.

The short or common seax was effectively a large knife (blade length 8-36cm), whose milieu was most probably the hunt (60). It was carried into battle and is shown on sculpture, see for example the Middleton warriors and the Repton Stone, purely as a sign of status. In combat it was definitely peripheral, a weapon of last resort, Beowulf is forced to use his 'slaughter-seax' because his sword his broken (*Beowulf* lines 2680-7, 2702-4 and 2904). The use of the word 'slaughter' to describe Beowulf's seax should not lead us to believe that it was actually an effective close-combat weapon – rather it describes it function, namely to dispatch, or as the poem puts it, to 'slaughter' wounded animals in the hunt and wounded enemies on the field of battle.

Bradbury's view, expounded in his work *The Battle of Hastings*, that the axe was a 'somewhat antique weapon' and thus the English's use of it was somewhat quaint and outdated is rather far from the truth. The axe if anything was in the flower of its manhood (61). For in England the axe was viewed as an effective cavalry weapon up until the mid-seventeenth century, and it was used by the Navy as a close-quarters weapon right through to the early nineteenth century.

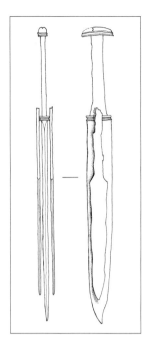

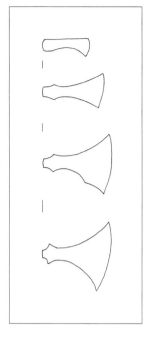

Far left: 60 An Anglo-Saxon hunting garniture. A seax and knife set from grave 93 Dover: Buckland. *Redrawn by M. Daniels from Evison 1987.*

Left: 61 Tenth- and eleventh-century axes. From top to bottom Wheeler Type I, IV, V & VI. *Redrawn by M. Daniels from Wheeler 1927.*

William of Poitiers tells us that at Hastings the English threw 'murderous axes' and one of the figures on the Bayeux Tapestry does appear to be mirroring William's words. There is, however, no reason to believe that these were the franciscas of the migration period. Instead we should see them as being axes of Wheeler Type I and IV. A rare late Anglo-Saxon manuscript illustration of an axe in combat, British Library *Ms. Cotton Cleopatra C VIII*, may be intended to show either a Wheeler Type IV or V, it could, however, represent the survival of an earlier style in that it resembles the axe-head found in grave 21 at Petersfinger in Wiltshire. The Petersfinger cemetery was in use from the fifth to the seventh century (*62, 63, 64* and *65*).

> Skarp-Hedin came swooping down on him and swung at him with his axe. The axe crashed down on his head and split it down to the jaw-bone, spilling the back-teeth on to the ice.
>
> *The Saga of Burnt Njal, 92*

Skarp-Hedin and his axe are one of the lasting images from the late thirteenth century *Njal's Saga*. Indeed in many ways they are archetypes – Skarp-Hedin is the perfect Viking, arrogant, fearless and axe wielding. As to the type of axe, well he was probably armed with something akin to the Mammen axe,

62 The axe in combat, from the eleventh-century British Library *Ms. Cotton Cleopatra C VIII.* The axe in question is very similar to the example from Petersfinger as illustated in figure 69. Also of note is the fact that the scabbard of the axe man's armoured opponent hangs from a belt or baldric which lies underneath his mail shirt.

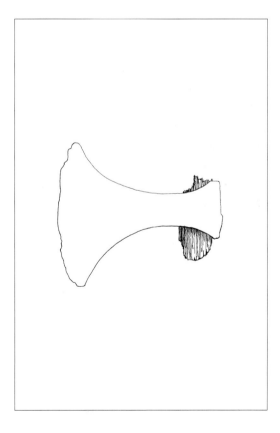

63 The axe from grave 21, Petersfinger, Wilts. Figures 58 and 62 point to the fact that there may have been a limited continuity of military equipment styles from the early to the late period in Anglo-Saxon England. *Redrawn by M. Daniels from Swanton 1973.*

64 The axe in combat, from the Bayeux Tapestry. The axe in question is very similar to the example from York as illustrated in figure 65.

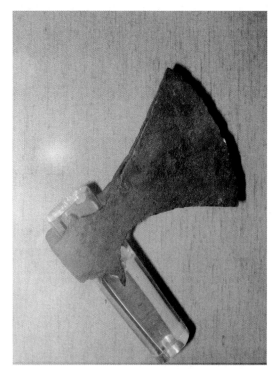

65 A late Viking period axe from York, in the Yorkshire Museum.

but in the popular imagination it would be the broad or Danish axe that he wielded.

The broad axe (Wheeler Type VI) first appeared around the year 1000, and was still in use, in England at least, as late as 1141, when at the Battle of Lincoln (according to John of Hexham) King Stephen wielded one with such skill and ferocity that he long held his foes at bay. As to the weapon itself a large (blade length on the curve ranged between approximately 19-25cm) yet surprisingly light head (the weight of a number of examples held in the collection of the Museum of London ranges between 15oz and 1lb11oz) was attached to a straight wooden shaft approximately 5ft in length (66 and 67). The lightness was achieved, as indeed Wheeler notes, by the surprising thinness of the blade, save at the socket and directly behind the edge. In a few cases decorative copper-alloy tubes lined the inside of the socket and extended someway down the haft. Such tubes should be viewed as decoration, and should not be confused with, nor viewed as an early form of the later medieval langets.

The use of the two-handed broad axe undoubtedly arose from the need to counteract two different tactical situations, one new the other rather old. The new situation was the increasing use, on the Continent at least, of armoured cavalry, the old situation, that was the need to break the symmetry of shield wall combat. The appearance of the broad axe around AD 1000 is slightly later, in equipment terms, than the first use of the kite shield and the conical helmet (in many ways the marks of the new armoured knight) and thus this new weapon may well be seen as an infantry response to the increasingly mounted continental warfare. The tenth-century Byzantine solution, or rather the latest Roman solution, to the problem of stiffening infantry facing an attack by heavy cavalry, was the *menavlion*, a long (2.7-3.6m) heavy spear. The weapon was designed to be thrust two-handed, and was a horse killer. The *menavlion* was in all probability known to the Vikings, yet as a tactical solution it was more fitted to the complex organisation of the Byzantine Army, which was in a position to field whole units of *menavlatoi*. The Vikings needed something less manpower intensive (something which could possibly be wielded by two or three members of a ship's crew), the solution was the broad axe. Horses will not charge into a solid body of formed infantry, rather they will come to a halt thus giving the men in the shield wall an opportunity to distract the rider while the axe-man steps through the rank and kills the horse. How easy this was to achieve in practise is hard to say, however, the initial success of the English at Hastings is worth remembering in this context.

As to its use in the clash of shield walls, well to understand the broad axe's role in that environment we must turn to the clash of the Swiss and their German counterparts, the Landskechts, during the Renaissance. Tactical symmetry occurs when two similarly equipped and trained armies clash. Such situations are observable in the Hellenistic period in the wars of the successor states, in the early Medieval

66 A tenth- or eleventh-century broad axe from the Thames, in the British Museum.

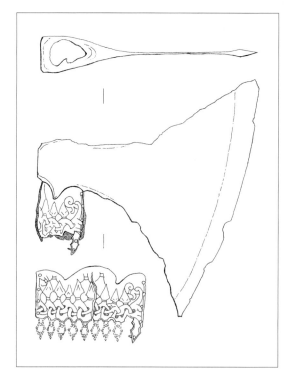

67 A broad axe with an ornamental socket, from Old London Bridge. *Redrawn by M. Daniels from Wheeler 1927.*

period in the clash of shield walls and in the clash of Renaissance pike formations. Formations, be they shield walls or pike blocks, collapse as a result of the creation of tears and gaps which are exploited to literally rip the enemy apart. The problem was – how to create the tears and gaps? In the case of Renaissance pike formations the solution arrived at was the *verlorne Haufe* ('lost outfit' or 'forlorn hope'), armed with halberds as well as hand-and-a-half and two-handed swords, and advancing ahead of their own pikemen they would try to hack their way into and so disrupt the enemy's pikes. The resultant confusion caused by the *verlorne Haufe* being, in theory, successfully exploited by their own pikemen. While I am not advocating that English and Viking broad axe-men were some kind of Early Medieval 'forlorn hope', what I am arguing is that they fulfilled to some extent the same role; namely, they attempted to overcome the symmetry by hacking their way into the enemy shield wall, thus creating a tear or gap which when exploited would lead to the enemy's collapse (*68* and *69*).

68 The broad axe as a symbol of martial prowess. This figure, from the Bayeux Tapestry, represents Harold Godwinson just prior to his coronation.

69 The broad axe in use. An Anglo-Danish housecarl from the Bayeux Tapestry.

The changes which occurred to the sword, or rather the reasons behind these changes, set the pattern for our understanding of the spear in the late Anglo-Saxon period. Despite Brooks attempt (in his 1991 paper *Weapons and Armour*) to furnish the English at Maldon with Swanton type spearheads, it is in fact far more likely that such weapons were the weapons of Byrhtnoth's ancestors, rather than of Byrhtnoth himself. For whilst it is likely that the English warriors who fought in the First Viking Age were armed with 'Swanton' spearheads, it is equally likely that their descendant who fought at Maldon, Ashingdon and Hastings, were not.

Instead we should look to the tenth- and eleventh-century finds from the River Thames (*70, 71* and *72*). Here we see both Viking (Petersen Types G, K and M) and Carolingian 'winged' spearheads. The main break with the past in

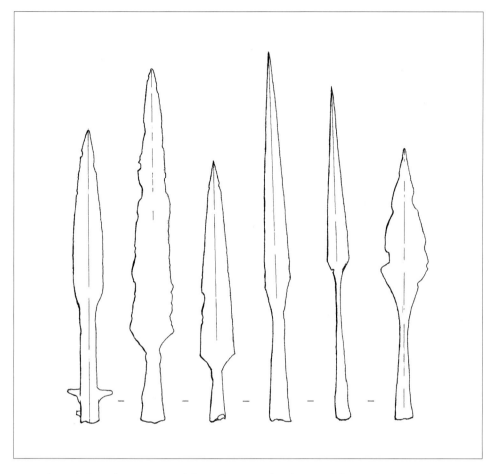

70 Tenth- and eleventh-century English or Viking spearheads. From left to right they are from Wandsworth, near Hampton Court, Walthamstom, Putney, Millbank near Tate Britain, and Datchet.

terms of construction being the "almost universal" (to quote Wheeler) adoption of the closed socket. As for head shapes, angular forms predominated, although 'leaf-bladed' examples, such as the Carolingian 'winged' type, were still used. Apart from the cosmetic change, and really today the change from Swanton's English types to Petersen's Viking types is what it has become, for there was nothing fundamentally wrong with the earlier English types, nor were the later Viking styles intrinsically better. However, at the end of the day it comes down to more than the simple question of actual effectiveness, perceived effectiveness and the copying of successful armies also enters the equation - thus Viking types replaced Anglo-Saxon types. But apart from that the spear remained essentially the same. Indeed it was in its essential, potentially, unchanged form since the days of ancient Greece.

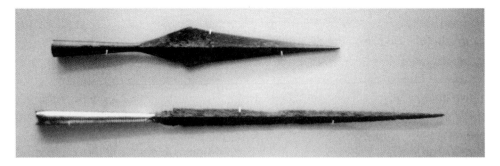

71 Two Viking period (tenth-eleventh century) spearheads from the London area in the British Museum. The socket on the shorter of the two is decorated with silver inlay, while twisted silver and copper wires were used to decorate the socket on the longer example.

72 Two 'winged' Carolingian style spearheads in the British Museum.

Finds from the Viking cemetery of Birka point to spear lengths of between 1.8m and 3.5m, with the majority being between 2.2-2.4m in length, the Birka finds are very similar to earlier extant examples from Illerup and Nydam, which measured between 2.23m and 3.54m, as well as to even earlier Greek and La Tène finds. Earlier Anglo-Saxon finds from Mucking appear to have been between 1.85m and 2.8m long. We should, therefore, expect late Anglo-Saxon spearheads to conform to Birka's 1.8-3.5m range. Questions we have difficulty in answering in relation to late Anglo-Saxon spears relate to the attachment of the head to the shaft, spear shaft decoration and the existence of the butt-spike.

In the case of earlier Roman and Germanic finds (see for example the spears from the Nydam bog deposit), both the spearhead and butt-spike, were when attached to the shaft, fitted to a whittled point which was stepped to accommodate the socket and provide a nice clean line. Whether this practice was followed in Anglo-Saxon England is harder to say. It appears to be show in the eighth-century Durham Cassiodrus manuscript illustration of *David as Victor*, and on the spears carried by the Viking Period Sockburn and Middleton warriors, as well as on a metalworker's die from Öland. But in all of these cases we may simply be seeing artistic simplification. Archaeologically, the phenomenon is possibly seen on the spearhead found in grave 55 at the Sewerby inhumation cemetery. Even here, however, the practice cannot be confirmed as the surviving fragment of spearshaft contained within the socket is fragmentary. Thus stepping may have been practised or it may not, it could well have been a case of personal preference.

We simply do not know if the Anglo-Saxons followed the Roman practice of painting their spear shafts – there is an absence of evidence, thus we are unable to either support or refute painting. However, remembering Vegetius' (*Epitome Rei Militaris* II.14) 'the glitter of arms strikes very great fear in the enemy', and the general gaudy, showy nature of the English warrior aristocracy, it would be surprising if they did not have painted spear shafts. As to continuance of Kragehul style shaft decoration, this appears to have been not so much discontinued as transferred from the shaft to the socket of the spearhead (*colour plate 11*). The adoption of the closed tubular socket, which provided a clear unbroken surface, probably led to this change. Surviving examples tended to use silver inlay to further ornament and enhance their elaborate interlace patterns:

> Giving him a mortal wound with his spear and adding yet another thrust with the lower end of it, he slew the tyrant hand to hand.

> Polybius, *The Histories*, XI.18.4

The butt-spike, the spears other head, was a Greek invention. As an important part of a hoplite's equipment it was near universal in the Greek phalanx, universal in the Roman Army and, from the archaeological evidence, very common in the Early Anglo-Saxon period. Despite the fact that the tactical picture, close-order infantry combat with spear and shield, remained unchanged. In the Anglo-Viking world the butt-spike in both archaeological and representational terms barely registers. It remained common in the Byzantine and Islamic worlds, yet we scrabble around to find rare examples such as the ninth-century Viking example from the Kilmainham-Islandbridge cemetery outside of Dublin. Now it may be that given the butt-spike's small size, compared to the spearhead, fewer have survived in the archaeological record. Equally, given the fact that they do not appear to have been as common in the early Anglo-Saxon world as they were in the Greco-Roman, it is possible that overtime they fell more and more into disuse and had disappeared entirely by the end of the Anglo-Saxon period. In tactical terms this would mean that when the spearhead broke off then either the broken shaft continued to be used, or else the broken spear was dropped and the sword was drawn (*73*).

73 A butt-spike from the Dover, Buckland Anglo-Saxon cemetery, in the British Museum. These 'second' spearheads, although common in the early Anglo-Saxon period seem to have fallen out of fashion by, and are rare, in both Western art and archaeology of the tenth and eleventh centuries.
They remain, however, a feature of Byzantine military equipment.

Moving now onto missile weapons we must now turn our attention to the bow (including the crossbow), the javelin, rocks, and the sling. The axe, as a missile, has already been discussed.

The *Maldon* poet tells us that in battle "bows were busy" (*The Battle of Maldon* line 110), yet how effective was the archery of the period? Previous studies of warfare have always been more concerned with determining the degree of use of the weapon, particularly in the late Anglo-Saxon period, as opposed to the range and the effectiveness of archery (see chapter 3 for a discussion on the use, or otherwise, of archers in the late Anglo-Saxon Army). Part of the reason for this derives from the fact that the true effectiveness of archery is, due to the number of variables at work, difficult to ascertain. The range is governed both by the calibre of the bow and by the strength of the archer, whilst as Coulston has correctly argued:

… the nature of the target, its size, vulnerability, rate of movement etc., also governs accuracy and effectiveness over various ranges.

The range of the bow in Anglo-Saxon England is unknown. Although the finds from Chessell Down on the Isle of Wight, and Bifrons, as well as the bog deposits of Nydam, Thorsbjerg and Vimose all show that the English, and their ancestors, employed the longbow (so named, it should be noted, to distinguish it from the crossbow. The so called 'short-bow' is a myth). However, even though the range of the weapon cannot be determined, its probable effectiveness can. Three pieces of evidence allow us to ascertain the probable effectiveness, if not the effective range of, the arrows of the period. These pieces of evidence are: the type of arrowheads used, the lid of the Franks Casket and the descriptions of the weapon in *Beowulf* and *The Battle of Maldon*.

Anglo-Saxon arrowheads fall into one of two types; they are either leaf-bladed (e.g. Berinsfield grave 150/5), or trilobate (e.g. Chessell Down grave 26). Manley states that:

Anglo-Saxon arrowheads *per se*, are unlikely to provide much insight into Saxon bowmanship.

Yet arrowheads do provide information on bowmanship, albeit indirectly, in that they define both the perceived target areas and the probable penetrative power of the arrow. The absence of bodkin heads and the use of leaf-bladed and trilobate heads points to their role in battle being an anti-personnel one, as opposed to an armour piercing one. In the case of both leaf-bladed and trilobate heads, the edge takes predominance over the point; this is in order to maximise the level of damage when shooting at soft targets. Their primary function was thus to cause deep penetrating wounds and massive haemorrhaging. Although at extreme close range, and shooting with a flat trajectory, such arrowheads as were used by the Anglo-Saxons may well have also been able to function in an armour piercing role.

This interpretation, of an anti-personnel as opposed to an armour piercing role for archery, is supported by both the representational and literary evidence. The lid of the Franks Casket depicts what Wilson describes as 'a lost Old English legend concerning Egil'. The scene is of a man defending his hall with bow and arrow. The Casket is believed to be of Northumbrian manufacture and has been dated to the first half of the eighth century. The various items of military equipment depicted on the Franks Casket are believed to reflect accurately the equipment and fashions of the day. It is thus considered a credible source from which to determine the effectiveness of archery against both armoured and shielded warriors.

The figure (the fifth from the left) that has most obviously succumbed to the archery is unarmoured. Although no shield was depicted with this attacker, this does not pose a problem as the figure fourth from the left is depicted using a shield. This figure (fourth from the left) appears to be wearing body armour, probably a mail shirt, and is advancing, crouched behind his shield. The shield, although hit by two arrows, is depicted as being proof against this form of attack, as only the tips of the points of the arrows are shown to penetrate the shield, whilst most of the arrow projects outwards from the board. This image, of the effectiveness of the shield against arrows, and thus the anti-personnel nature of Anglo-Saxon archery, is further reinforced by the poetry.

Beowulf (lines 3114-3119) states that warriors could be felled by arrows, but only by those arrows which passed over the shield wall, thus implying that the shield wall was an effective defence against arrows. Whilst *The Battle of Maldon* (lines 265-72), describing the contribution made by the Northumbrian Aescferth, states that he shot many arrows some of which found their mark, 'sometimes he ripped open a man'.

Before considering the effectiveness of the javelin, a mention must be made of the crossbow. It is believed that crossbows are depicted on a number of Pictish stones, although this interpretation has recently been questioned. Comparisons can also be drawn (although none have been) between the weapons depicted on the Pictish stones and the late Roman/Byzantine *solenarion* or arrow-guide. Roman depictions of the crossbow are also not as unambiguous as Coulston believes, and as with the Pictish examples, the two third-century Gallo-Roman reliefs which purport to show crossbows more probably depict composite bows and arrow-guides. Whatsoever is the case, it impacts not at all on the current discussion as in all cases the weapon is shown in a purely hunting context and there is no mention of the crossbow in an Anglo-Saxon military context prior to its use by the Normans during the invasion of AD 1066. Indeed, if we view the crossbow more as a weapon suited to siege warfare, then its use by the Normans and not by the English becomes more understandable.

The arrowheads of the period were solely anti-personnel in nature, the same was also true of the javelins used during the same period. The big changes in javelin design from the early period being that the armour piercing styles seem to have been abandoned, plus alongside the socket angular and leaf-bladed varieties we now also see Viking tanged angular and barbed styles (*74* and *75*). Indeed *The Battle of Maldon*, which of all the surviving poems emphasises the spear over the sword, describes the use of javelins solely in an anti-personnel capacity (*The Battle of Maldon* lines 134-158). However, Dickinson and Härke believe that at close range the shield board would have been compromised by missiles, and in this belief they are supported by experimental evidence. Griffiths and Sim have demonstrated that authentically reconstructed Roman leaf-bladed javelins can, at a range of 10m, penetrate 18mm of oak and project their points 10mm through the back of the wood. However, they conclude by stating that, 'such javelins were of little use against a body of close-order infantry.'

In support of this conclusion they cite Onasander who, in his work *The General*, (XIX.2), recommends the use of javelins against a unit's flanks, which are unprotected by shields. This apparent dichotomy of opinion is, however, more perceived than actual. Griffiths and Sim are correct in following Onasander, for javelins, like all weapons are far more effective against unarmoured targets, and indeed this, unsurprisingly, appears to have been understood by the Anglo-Saxons. However, Dickinson and Härke are also undoubtedly correct in their conclusion. At close range, 10m or less, these weapons do appear to have had the potential to function in an armour piercing capacity, even though they were not specifically designed to act in this capacity.

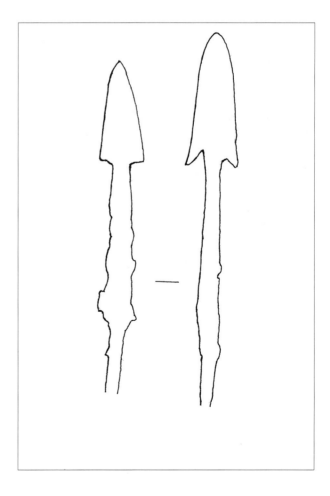

74 Typical tanged Viking javelin heads.

75 A socketed javelin, no date, but universal in design. *From St. Paul's in Jarrow.*

Two missile weapons which have not so far been considered are the sling and the hand-thrown stone, neither of which may have been used militarily in the period under study. The latter can be easily discounted as hand-thrown stones are primarily a weapon of siege warfare, although the use of stones in battle is known in the Roman period (Dio LXXV.6). The only possible mention of their use by Anglo-Saxons comes from a description of the battle of Hastings in the eleventh century by William of Poitiers, in which he states that, the English 'threw spears and weapons of every kind, murderous axes and stones tied to sticks.'

However, as this statement is the closest description that exists for the use of hand-thrown stones in the whole of the Anglo-Saxon period, it seems unlikely that they were regularly used as a weapon by the Anglo-Saxons.

As for the sling, although Harrison believes that the sling may have been used on the battlefield by the Anglo-Saxons, the evidence for such an assertion is slight. The use of the sling in an agricultural context, specifically in a bird scaring or killing role, is attested by two similar illustrations: one is British Library, *Ms. Cotton Claudius B.IV* and the other is in the lower margin of the Bayeux Tapestry. Militarily, the tenth- or eleventh-century British Library *Ms. Harley 603* shows a slinger engaging an armoured opponent. The value of the illustration, in British Library *Ms. Harley 603*, is lessened due to the fact that the scene in question shows David fighting Goliath; a sling is thus *de rigueur*, and its use in the illustration is in all probability more a reflection of the subject matter, as opposed to a depiction of the realities of the warfare of the period of the manuscript. The literary evidence for the use of the sling comes from one of Aldhelm's riddles and from Eddius Stephanus' *Life of Wilfrid*. Eddius Stephanus, in his eighth-century work the *Life of Wilfrid*, appears more concerned with drawing biblical parallels than with reflecting the realities of warfare. Indeed, in the passage in question, apart from the sling, no other weapon is mentioned by Eddius Stephanus, despite the fact that the use of the sling precipitates a battle. Whilst Eddius Stephanus' description of the use of the sling by one of Bishop Wilfrid's companions is possibly intended to be more metaphorical than real:

> The chief priest of their idolatry set himself up on a high mound like Balaam and started to curse God's people, trying to bind their hands by his magic art. One of the bishop's companions took a stone which all the people of God had blessed, and hurled it like David from a sling. It pierced the wizard's forehead through to the brain. Death took him as it took Goliath, unawares, and he fell back lifeless on the sand.

Aldhelm, writing either in the seventh or early eighth century, could be said to follow Eddius Stephanus, in that although the sling is the answer to one of his riddles, that answer:

> ... almost certainly only refers to the weapon used by David to slay Goliath.

> DeVries 1992, *Medieval Military Technology*

Thus, given the fact that the only evidence for the military use of the sling in the Anglo-Saxon period is very much centred around the story of David and Goliath, it is unlikely that it was used as a weapon by the Anglo-Saxons.

HERIOTS AND THE COMPLETE WARRIOR

What are, or rather were, *heriots*? *Heriots* (from *here-geatu* or war–gear) were a form of death-duty. For for all those of thegnly rank or above, on their death they were required to arrange for the payment of a set quantity of military equipment to their lord. Although the payment could be remitted to cash, and usually was in the Danelaw, in general, military equipment was paid, with the level or amount being determined by rank.

Thus in II Cnut 71 an earl's *heriot* consisted of 8 horses (4 saddled, 4 unsaddled), 4 helmets, 4 byrines (mail shirts), 4 swords, 8 spears, 8 shields and 200 *mancuses* of gold; a king's thegn was expected to pay 4 horses (2 saddled, 2 unsaddled), 1 helmet, 1 byrine, 2 swords, 4 spears, 4 shields and 50 *mancuses* of gold; while a lesser thegn paid 1 saddled horse plus one each of helmet, byrine, sword, spear and shield, as well as a lesser amount of money. In the Danelaw, according to II Cnut 71, the *heriots* of a king's thegn with soke and of a lesser thegn were simple money payments (£4 and £2 respectively); only a king's thegn closer to the king was expected to supply arms as well, specifically 2 horses (1 saddled, 1 unsaddled), 1 sword, 2 spears, 2 shields and 50 *mancuses* of gold.

How then do we interpret II Cnut 71, which is, it must be remembered corroborated, in level of payment terms by surviving late Anglo-Saxon wills.

Heriots as set amounts of money or military equipment (arms, armour and horses) plus money dependant upon rank, may have simply been related to rank and the deceased's ability to pay; and as with earlier grave goods, have been, or should be seen as, simply symbolic of rank and status. They should thus (following this explanation) not be equated to the actual military equipment carried by the various ranks or levels of society into battle. This explanation, although possible, is not terribly plausible. The usual view that *heriots* represented the battlefield equipment of the various levels of society engaged in warfare remains the most likely interpretation, however, the question remains – what is the key?

Brooks (in his *Communities and Warfare 700-1400*) believes that the 'most probable' reconstruction for the earl's *heriot* is 'for four fully armed soldiers (each with helmet, byrine, sword, spear, shield and saddled horse) and four attendants armed only with spear and shield.' The problem with Brooks' interpretation are the four attendants (whom he muses may have been grooms and may have ridden the unsaddled horse bareback, equally the unsaddled horse may have been reliefs or pack-horses).

The *attendants* take us to the heart of the problem – namely what constituted a viable weapon set? Was a spear and shield enough? Were the attendants, if they existed and if they were so armed, viable? The answer to these latter two questions is an emphatic *no*. Whilst we know that Anglo-Saxon armies had a logistic train (see Bede, *Historia Ecclesiastica*, IV.22 and the story of Imma) there was no need for it to be armed, that was not its job, and there was certainly no need for it to be badly armed. For anyone armed simply with spear and shield was not only unviable, they were a positive liability. Why? Because they lacked either an axe or a sword. The Maldon poet rightly stresses the importance of the spear in Anglo-Saxon warfare, but at some point the fighting would come down to the edge of a sword. Anyone not equipped for this stage of battle (with sword or axe) was a liability in both physical and morale terms.

Thus the minimum viable weapons set was – a shield, and a spear, and a sword. Even in that closest of close-order formations, the Macedonian pike phalanx, every man carried a sword. Nor were the Macedonians in any way unique, rather they were the norm, and their equipment (pike, shield, sword) a vital part of the way the game of Western warfare was played. Thus the Anglo-Saxons being a part of that game, that tradition, followed the rules laid down centuries before by the game's inventors the Greeks. The Anglo-Saxons fielded properly equipped forces. We are dealing here with the wars of aristocratic warrior elites and their armed followers, and in this context *heriots* were used to provide viable sets of military equipment. Thus the answer to the question – what was the key? The sword was the key, the number of swords equals the number of viable weapons sets and thus the number of men a *heriot* was designed to equip. Loyn in his *The Governance of Anglo-Saxon England 500-1087*, when speaking of *heriots*, states:

> The basic impression, however, is clear and sound. Earls and thegns were men magnificently equipped for the warfare of the age.

That is what we see when we look at II Cnut 71 and surviving Late Anglo-Saxon wills (*76, 77* and *78*). Yes attendants would have been present, but as unarmed servants, they would not have been equipped in such a way as to make them incapable of combat and thus liable to run away at the first hint of trouble. Thus in II Cnut 71 an earl's *heriot* equipped four armoured men, while that of a king's thegn equipped one body-armoured, and one unbody-armoured man. As for the extra shields and spears, in all of the cases where they occur we also have unsaddled horse. These horses would have probably doubled as both relief and pack-horse, and in the latter capacity they would have carried those things which all the evidence shows to have been somewhat fragile, definitely disposable, yet vital, namely (spare) shields and spears.

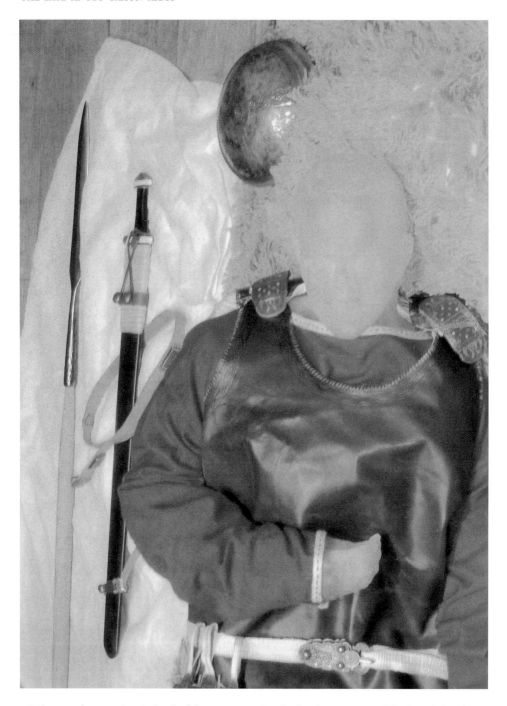

76 The complete warrior. A detail of the reconstruction, in the site museum, of the burial chamber. from mound 1 at Sutton Hoo.

Right: 77 The complete warrior.
A further detail of the reconstructed
Sutton Hoo mound 1 burial chamber.

Below: 78 The complete warrior or
warriors. The armoured knights from
the twelfth-century 'Temple Pyx'.
Their equipment does not differ
markedly from their earlier eleventh-
century counterparts.

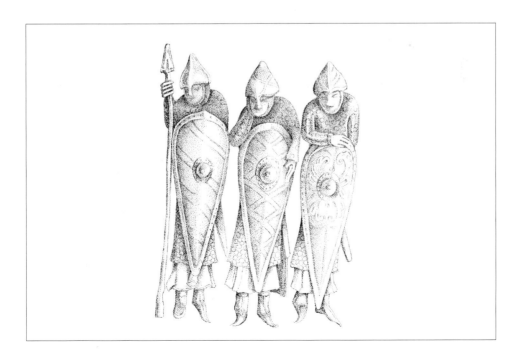

CHAPTER FIVE

BATTLE – MALDON, AD 991

In the dark watches of the night, a Viking raiding fleet unstepped their masts and began the long pull into the Blackwater Estuary. Their destination Northey Island (79). Their victim, the sleeping burgh of Maldon. Yet at some point, possibly as they passed the church set amidst the ruins of the great Roman fortifications at Bradwell they were espied and the alarm was raised. Thus on the morning of the 10 or the 11 August AD 991 (we cannot say for certain) the raiders found their landing contested by an English host led by one of the foremost men in the realm – Ealdorman Byrhtnoth (*colour plate 1*). The subsequent battle which ensued has since become famous, possibly out of all proportion to its actual significance.

Its fame rests upon the fact that it was the first great English defeat of the Second Viking Age, and given that it occurred at the start of the renewal of Viking activity it has at times been viewed by later commentators not only as a precursor to, but also the reason behind many of Aethelred's future problems and failures. Coupled with this is the death of Byrhtnoth in the battle, despite subsequent criticism of his folly and arrogance particularly in respect to his command decisions, his loss at such a crucial time has been viewed as a serious blow to Aethelredian England. Finally, its fame rests upon the survival of some 325 lines of poetry. The poem, which we know as *The Battle of Maldon*, is incomplete, as it lacks a beginning and an end, and even a title. Yet for all that the work, which was probably written just after the defeat, provides a realistic outline of the events of the engagement. As for the deaths described at the end of the poem, well they should be viewed in the light of the Duke of Wellington's 8 August 1815 correspondence to John Croker on the subject of describing the Battle of Waterloo, in which the Duke stated that, 'the history of a battle is not unlike the history of a ball.' Thus in the deaths of Byrthnoth's *duguth* and *geoguth* we are seeing a poetic rendering of the individual dances, rather than:

79 Northey Island as seen from the mainland.

The order in which, or the exact moments at which, they occurred.

Wellington to Croker, 8 August 1815

In the summer of the year 991 a Viking fleet ravaged the coast of England. Its first target, or victim, was Folkestone, next it attacked Sandwich. After Sandwich, well after Sandwich we see the real value of the warships of the period, namely strategic mobility. For the Vikings now left Kent and the south-east behind instead turning their attention to East Anglia they appeared suddenly at Ipswich. This type of warfare, raiding, or (to coin a later medieval term) a sort of naval *chevauchée*, is predicated on speed, surprise and the avoidance of battle, and these factors account for the Viking's decision to backtrack and attack Maldon. Equally, they have tended to be overlooked when considering the engagement which occurred outside Maldon, as indeed has the geography of Northey Island itself (far too much time has been spent staring at the causeway and in criticising Byrthnoth's *ofermod (80)*).

The Vikings undoubtedly knew both Maldon and Northey Island and would have chosen the island as a landing site for two reasons. Firstly the island is accessible only by boat or by the causeway at low tide, it thus provided the Vikings with a secure easily guarded landing site for their ships. Secondly, importantly, Northey Island is a hill, thus anyone landing on the eastern side of the island is nicely screened from Maldon by the hill which forms the western side of the island. Given this we are able to tentatively reconstruct the Viking's plan of attack, always bearing in mind that they were intending to raid and sack Maldon, not fight a pitched battle (*colour plates 12* and *13*).

80 The causeway, looking from the hill.

On the 10 and 11 August 2005, the causeway at Northey Island was completely clear at 6.30a.m. and 6.45a.m. respectively, and we should expect something similar for the same dates in 991; Scragg puts it at 4.43a.m. The Vikings would therefore have unstepped their masts at night, at sea and then pulled upstream to Northey Island in the darkness, intent upon using the island itself to cover their landing. Crossing the causeway, probably even before it was completely clear, either in the dark before dawn or in the grey light of dawn itself, they would have purposed to take the sleepy defenders of Maldon at unawares. They would not have wanted to attack manned fortifications. Malplaquet, fought on the 11 September 1709, described, for good reason, as a 'very murdering battle', was Marlborough's last great victory. It was also his most costly, and it shows how difficult and expensive in lives even field fortifications are to attack. It is even more 'murdering' to attack across ditches and walls which have not been filled and breached, in the face of a determined defence, far better to escalade a sleeping garrison.

Yet for the Vikings their plan miscarried — they were seen and not only was their target forewarned, but a force was available to intercept them on landing. It is unlikely that their intentions were divined upon leaving Ipswich as they would have been well out of site of land before they turned south towards Maldon. Rather they were probably spotted upon entering the Blackwater.

Now for the English we can see, what can only be described as the first stroke of luck. Naval warfare is a decidedly tricky and chancy affair, even as late as the twentieth century the bringing together of two opposing fleets has proved remarkably difficult and the prevention of raids has at times proved nigh on impossible. Even Rome, for all its wealth, power and martial prowess, was unable to prevent or suppress Saxon piracy from the third century onwards, Carausius, the Roman official turned usurper, charged with the task of ending such raids, observed that it was far easier, indeed it was at least possible, to intercept the pirates after the event rather than before it. Byrhtnoth's ability to bar the causeway we should therefore ascribe to luck rather than good judgement. Luck in that the Vikings were seen, luck in that not only did the intelligence reach Byrhtnoth in time but also in that he was able to both interpret it correctly and be close enough to Maldon and Northey Island to allow him to act upon it. The one factor in all of this which does not rely upon luck is the fact that Byrhtnoth and his host were probably already assembled in this area as a result of the earlier raids.

THE CAUSEWAY

We have reached what Sergeant Colon insists on calling an *imp* arse.

Terry Pratchett, *The Fifth Elephant*

The Vikings on disembarking pulled their ships up onto the flat east side of the island, arrayed themselves in their armour and passing along the south-east side of Northey Island, shielded by the hill, they made their way to the causeway to await the tide. Yet to their surprise they found a most unwelcome sight – an English army. From the poem (and in this chapter the poem, unless otherwise stated, is always *The Battle of Maldon*), lines 2-24, it appears that the English had themselves only just arrived and that the Vikings were able to watch as Byrhtnoth put his forces into array (*81* and *colour plates 15* and *16*). Horses where sent to the rear and the shield wall formed (see chapter 3 for a detailed discussion of the form and function of a shield wall). Byrhtnoth's advice, lines 18-21, on how to stand, how to hold the shield, is not, or rather was not as has at times ludicrously been stated, on the spot training. Rather in the Maldon poet's echoing of the seventh-century BC Greek elegiast Tyrtaeus' words:

Fear ye not a multitude of men, nor flinch, but let every man hold his shield straight towards the van.

81 The English end of the causeway. Byrhtnoth would have drawn up his troops near this spot in AD 991.

We are seeing no more than the mantra of Western close-order infantry combat – stand straight, stand steady, look to your front.

For the Vikings this turn of events would have been unexpected and unwelcome. Battles are dreadfully risky affairs, which can leave even the victors exhausted and badly damaged. We tend to view history as an 'age of battles', yet in truth that phrase really applies to the period from Breitenfeld onwards (1631 – to the present). For the Later Medieval period kings such as Henry II of England, his son, Richard I, and Philip Augustus of France made their name as great warriors not by literally risking all in the uncertainty of battle, rather success in sieges and on raids marked them out from their contemporaries.

The poem (lines 25-6) sees the raiders asking for and, understandably, being refused tribute. Now this section of the poem is easy to view in the light of later payments – yet more fundamental is the assumption that at this point battle was inevitable. Why was this so? Yes we know that a battle did take place, but everyone has been so hung up on Byrhtnoth's generalship and of course his *ofermod*, that no one ever questions the Viking's actions. To the question of the Vikings actions we will return in due course when we consider the shield wall phase of the battle and the reasons behind Byrhtnoth's decision to allow the Vikings to cross the causeway.

The demand for tribute may well have been genuine. The Vikings had everything to gain and nothing to lose by such a demand. Equally, the English refusal seen in the light of earlier events – namely the Alfredian success and the subsequent unification of England – will have given the English no pause for doubt in dismissing out of hand the Vikings request for silver. As for the numbers involved, well the *Anglo-Saxon Chronicle* A manuscript speaks of 93 ships, as for the English, suffice it to say Byrhtnoth was an experienced soldier and probably believed, indeed he probably possessed, the numbers to do the job. And that is as much of the numbers game as I am minded to play – for make no mistake it is a game, and one for which we lack sufficient evidence to draw exact, or even near exact conclusions, in order to reach a satisfactory answer.

Separated still by 'the waters of the Pante' both sides engaged in ineffectual sniping, certainly with bows but also probably with javelins. Once the causeway became clear, or at least crossable, Byrhtnoth seized the initiative. Putting a force onto the causeway the English effectively blocked the Vikings, trapping them on the island, but as will be seen it was a trap with no jaws. Wulfstan and his two companions Ælfhere and Maccus, were, like the great hero Horatius in Macaulay's *Lays of Ancient Rome*, in a strong position. Their flanks were secure, the mud on either side of the causeway is deep and clinging, making movement through it, in military terms, impossible (*colour plate 14*). Even if the Vikings attempted to wade through the mud, and we have no evidence or reason to suppose that they did, then they would have found the crossing slow, exhausting and disruptive to any formation, and they would have arrived at the English held bank exhausted and piecemeal and would have died exhausted and piecemeal. The causeway was the only way across, yet it was easily blocked by a small force – neither side could properly engage the other – a state of impasse had been reached.

SHIELD WALL

> They [the Vikings] asked to be allowed to have passage
> to cross over the ford, to advance their troops
>
> *The Battle of Maldon,* lines 87–8

Then Byrhtnoth, because of his *ofermod*, his over weaning pride, his over confidence, pulled back his forces and allowed the Vikings passage of the causeway. Now we come to reasons, to ask why, why did Byrhtnoth allow the Vikings to cross? And why did the Vikings seek battle?

Byrhtnoth's motives are the easiest to fathom. He had done the impossible, he had intercepted the force that had ravaged Folkestone, Sandwich and Ipswich before they attacked their next target. However, his triumph was hollow for he could not bring them to battle. Only by defeating them in battle and destroying their forces could Byrhtnoth end the raids, not only now but also potentially in the future by sending a message that England, or at least this part of England, was well defended and that similar adventures would end the same way. Byrhtnoth, therefore, had little choice if he was to fight the battle he had planned to fight then the Vikings had to be allowed to cross to the mainland. Byrhtnoth's decision therefore had nothing to do with *ofermod*, instead it had everything to do with the reality of the situation facing him. As for *ofermod*, despite Tolkien's damning indictment of it, in an aristocratic warrior milieu was it not rather a virtue, as opposed to the fault it is usually portrayed as. Where not all the great figures of Anglo-Saxon literature and history, Beowulf, Finn, Edgar with his second coronation, his imperial coronation, at Bath, even Alfred when his piety allowed it, not to some extent *ofermod*. Pride, arrogance, swagger were possessed by all of the great commanders of history. These character traits, which in civilian life are seen as unappealing, are in military life viewed at times as something akin to virtues — particularly, as was the case in Anglo-Saxon England, in an age of heroic leadership. They are a way a leader exudes confidence both in himself and in his men, they are morale building and boosting and as those great *ofermod* commanders Napoleon and Montgomery noted — morale wins battles.

What then of the Vikings? The Vikings were conducting a campaign of raiding, pitched battles were not, so to speak, on their 'to do' list, indeed they where to be avoided at all costs. Why then did they seek to cross the causeway?

The Vikings where faced with a number of problems, and in military intelligence terms they could not see over the hill, they were merely in a position to guess what was on the other side of it. As Pullen-Appleby pointed out in his 2005 study *English Sea Power,* the Anglo-Saxon's preferred tactic for dealing with a raiding force such as the one currently languishing on Northey Island was to pin it between a land and a naval force. The Vikings undoubtedly knew this and may well have been expecting English warships to make an appearance as soon as conditions, namely the tide, were favourable. There non-appearance at this stage presented the Vikings with an opportunity to defeat the force in front of them before having to deal with any new threat if and/or when it should appear. It would be better to fight concurrent battles than to face two enemy forces simultaneously from different directions. Of course we do not know if Byrhtnoth was expecting naval support. Maybe he was and it had failed to appear, maybe he knew it would not arrive in time to help decide the issue, or may be there was none available. Whatever the case, upper-most in the mind of each of the commanders was the question of escape. Byrhtnoth could not afford to let the Vikings escape as he could not be certain that he would ever bring them to battle again. As for the Vikings, I believe that they did not see escape without battle as an option, and if they were going to have to fight then now was the best time, for the longer they sat there the likelier it was that the forces arrayed against them, both on land and also possibly at sea, would increase to such a point so as to make victory and thus any chance of escape, impracticable.

Crossing the causeway:

… the sailors carried their lime-wood shields on to the land.
There against the fierce ones stood ready
Byrhtnoth with his men. He commanded that with the shields
They form the shield wall, and that the company hold out
Firm against the fiends. Then the fight was near.

The Battle of Maldon, lines 99-103

At this point a further exchange of missiles occurred, then the two sides closed to contact (*82* and *colour plate 17*).

The dynamics of shield wall combat and the presence or absence of body-armour in the English ranks has already been considered and discussed at some length earlier in this work (see below, chapters 3 and 4 respectively). Therefore, rather than go over the issues and reiterate the evidence, we shall instead examine the event that broke the symmetry of the shield wall and decisively settled the combat – namely the death of Byrhtnoth.

How soon it occurred after the shield walls collided is impossible say, as far as we are concerned the cataclysmic event occurred between lines 162 and 182. Heroic leadership and the death in battle of the leader need not, given the correct set of circumstances, prove fatal to a side's chances of winning. Consider, for example, Wolfe at Quebec, or for that matter the case of Lieutenant Colonel H. Jones at Goose Green in the Falklands. In the latter case at least we see the death of the leader as a spur to victory. However, in the main it is not to be recommended. The death of Epaminondas at Mantinea in 362 BC proved fatal for the Thebans, while the mere belief that William was dead very nearly proved disastrous for the Norman cause at Hastings.

Hindsight, possessed by ourselves and the poet, has in a way distorted our view of the events of that day in August. Even the surviving opening half-line of the poem '… would be broken' seems to taunt us with the inevitability of

82 The site of the battle, with Northey Island in the background. Of note, other than the hill, is the island's flat eastern side stretching out into the Blackwater.

the English defeat. While, all too often, in the twentieth century, Byrhtnoth has been transformed into a stereotypical First World War general or Colonel Blimp type figure whose *ofermod* came before his fall. Indeed, it is very easy in this light to see the Viking's saying (to re-quote that great unattributable quote) – 'The English soldiers fight like lions. True. But don't we know that they are lions led by donkeys'.

Yet to view events in this light would be wrong, for up until his death, everything, as far as Byrhtnoth was concerned, seemed to be going right, his strategy, such as we can glean that it was working. Although it was, it must be admitted, combined with a little luck, but then Napoleon and Frederick the Great would have understood that. Byrhtnoth was lucky to have intercepted the Vikings before they sacked Maldon, his luck held in that he was able, despite the problems of the terrain, to bring them to battle. His luck failed in the bloody constraint of battle. But then, as has already been pointed out, battles are risky ventures.

THE COLLAPSE

Then did the lack-willed leave the battlefield.

The Battle of Maldon, line 185

Whilst Byrhtnoth's death provided the catalyst for the English defeat, it was ironically the belief that he was alive that broke the shield wall and put the better part of the *fyrd* into flight.

Byrhtnoth died fighting in the centre of the English line, with his household around him. Then, like unto a scene taken straight out of the *Iliad,* a fight developed over his body and his armour, in the course of which both Ælfnoth and Wulfmær, who stood beside their lord were also slain (*The Battle of Maldon,* lines 182-3). Even in the midst of this Homeric contest the English cause was not necessarily lost, for by its very nature close-order infantry combat shielded the ealdorman's death from the majority of his men. Yet here, in this death, we see one of the flaws of heroic leadership, for those who saw it, it had an immediate morale effect. For some, and we will return to this point in a moment, it spurred them, so the poet would have us believe, onto great deeds. On others it had quite the opposite effect.

If the best of us is dead what chance have we lesser mortals – may well sum up the attitude of those who 'departed from the battlefield' (*The Battle of Maldon,* line 185). The trickling of men away from the fighting, if the process began in this fashion, and line 185 of the poem appears to have implied that it did, would certainly not have gone unnoticed by the rest of the English line, and it practically goes without saying that the effect would have been unsettling. The trickling turned into a flood when 'Godric quit the field' (*The Battle of Maldon* , line 187), for in his haste to escape he took Byrhtnoth's horse. This fateful horse was undoubtedly not only the best mount present, but was also, importantly, the most recognisable:

… too many men believed, when he rode away on the horse,
on the prancing steed, that it was our lord:
because of that the army became fragmented here on the battlefield,
the shield-wall smashed to pieces. Blast his action,
that he should have put so many men to flight here.

The Battle of Maldon, lines 239-43

Thus it was the belief that Byrhtnoth was alive, possibly wounded, but definitely alive and fleeing the field that brought ruin to the English cause that day. Not, ironically, his death. Indeed it is possible, had all his household, and Godric and his brothers were a part of Byrhtnoth's household, proved true, that the English may yet have prevailed and won the day. But it was not to be.

It appears that the flanks of the Anglo-Saxon host disintegrated, leaving the remains (those who were neither dead nor fled) of the centre, the household troop, still engaged with the enemy. From this point on (line 202) the poem deals with Wellington's grim heroic dances – the individual deaths of Byrhtnoth's *comitatus*. We are now left with the final big question of the poem and the events of the battle, namely the deaths of the retainers and the question of men dying with their lord.

On a purely practical level it must be remembered that disengagement and retirement in the face of the enemy is one of the hardest tricks to pull off. The centre of the English line was probably the most heavily engaged, it may even have been driving the Vikings back, and in such circumstances disengagement would have been impossible. In which case the final part of the poem may be viewed simply as a case of putting a heroic gloss over the military realities of the situation. Equally, and to a large extent supporting this view is the argument advanced by Woolf and Frank that the ideal of men dying with their lord is nothing more than a late Anglo-Saxon literary construct not grounded in the reality of either the age or the warfare of the age.

Yet such views can to some degree be described as cynical, relying too much on a post-modern rationalisation of the sources and not giving enough credence to the *mores* of an heroic, aristocratic warrior elite. Societies are governed by rules, by codes of behaviour, even if at times such codes are observed more in the breach than in the observance. The problem with trying to understand the ideal of men dying with their lord in battle is the evidence. For it is mentioned by Tacitus, in the first century AD, in his *Germania*, as well as by Caesar and Sallust. However, for Anglo-Saxon England we have to jump to the eighth century and the failed *coup d'état* of Cyneheard, in 755. From there we move forward again to *The Battle of Maldon*. Moving slightly sideways we must also consider *the Fight at Finnsburg*, the 'episode' in Beowulf, as well as Wiglaf's actions in *Beowulf*.

> Never was the bright mead better earned
> than that which Hnaef gave his guard of youth.

The Fight at Finnsburg, lines 39-40

In the gift-counter-gift culture that we see in *Beowulf, Finnsburg, Maldon*, indeed which is portrayed throughout the whole of Anglo-Saxon literature, service is unto death. The question is of course did such service, the bonds of lordship extend beyond the death in battle of the lord? The heroic ideal answer was – yes. Wiglaf upbraids his companions for not following his example and going to the aid of Beowulf, even though the eponymous hero may well have been wounded unto death. Hengist, despite Finn's hospitality, sees that his duty and honour require him to avenge Hnaef.

As for Maldon, in stark prosaic terms I do not believe that Byrhtnoth's *comitatus* were in any position to disengage from the Vikings. Equally they were not cowards, and whilst they undoubtedly had a realistic view of their situation, they were also the product of their society. Their, background, training, and upbringing was aristocratic, heroic and martial. Given the situation they could do nothing less than to fight and die to avenge their lord. Indeed, their very education had taught them that this was, in these circumstances, both right and proper.

To the victors – escape. The price of victory was it appears too high for anything else. There is nothing bloodier than two Western armies facing each other in battle. We lack casualty figures for the engagement, but maybe, indeed it appears likely that the English force, particularly the last stand of Byrhtnoth's household, exacted a heavy toll before they themselves were destroyed. As for Maldon itself, it escaped sack, so Byrhtnoth at least succeeded in one respect.

However, the preservation of Maldon and the possibility of heavy Viking casualties cannot detract from the fact that this was anything other than a defeat for the English. A defeat made all the worse by the death in the battle of one of the country's leading men. The failure to use naval forces to interdict the now weakened raiders, combined with the 'buying of peace' and the departure of the Vikings merely served to compound the extent of the defeat.

CHAPTER SIX

CAMPAIGN – 1066 THE WAR OF THE ENGLISH SUCCESSION

With cheerless spirits they bewailed their soul's sorrow, the death of their leader. Likewise, a Geatish woman, sorrowful, her hair bound up, sang a mournful lay, chanted clamorously again and again that she sorely feared days of lamentation for herself, a multitude of slaughters, the terror of an army, humiliation and captivity.

Beowulf, lines 3148-3155

Major success in a surprise action therefore does not depend on the energy, forcefulness, and resolution of the commander: it must be favoured by other circumstances. We do not wish to deny the possibility of success, but merely want to establish the fact that it does require favourable conditions, which are not often present, and can rarely be created by the general.

von Clausewitz, *On War*, bk.3 ch.9

If we are to apportion blame for the succession crisis of 1066 then we need look no further than the person of the dead king.

Starkey, in his work on Elizabeth I, notes that exile prior to accession breeds flaws. In the case of Henry VII, 'a corrosive and destructive suspicion; [in] Charles II's [case] an equally corrosive cynicism.' In Edward the Confessor, who incidentally needs adding to Starkey's list, it bred a corrosive myopia, a desire for immediate advantage and survival with little or no thought to the future, and this attitude is no where better seen than in the question of the succession.

Edward and Edith, his queen, came from fecund families, and although the mysteries of human reproduction are only now being fully unravelled, at this remove of time there appears on the surface at least every reason for contemporaries to have expected issue from the union. Of course if John is correct in asserting that Edward had sworn a vow of chastity then the question of fertility or the lack of it, is moot. Equally if Edward swore such a vow then Maitland's view of him as a 'holy simpleton' has some merit. Scyld Scefing – 'That was a great king!' (*Beowulf*, line 11) – his great king status, as proclaimed in line 11 of the poem, stemmed primarily from his success in warfare. It also in part derived from the fact that he left a worthy successor – his son Beowulf (not the eponymous hero). Beowulf Sylding in his turn, so the poet tells us, begat heirs. Kingship in the eleventh century differed little from kingship in earlier and indeed later centuries, true the late Anglo-Saxon State was larger and more complex than the conquest kingdoms of the sixth century, but at the end of the day a king was still expected to be the shield of his people and to fulfil his dynastic imperative role – heirs and spares.

One would have thought that the dynamic pressure upon Edward, the momentum to continue the line of kings, would have been unstoppable. For Edward was of the House of Cerdic, whose regnal list stretched back 500 years in Wessex and beyond on the Continent to Woden himself. Yet for all that he failed to produce offspring, either legitimate or illegitimate, and as Harold I Harefoot had shown, questions of legitimacy were no bar to the acquisition of royal power. The reason, behind Edward's actions, appears to have been a short-term view of life, which was in itself probably a result of his years of exile. A noble exile, without land or followers, relies entirely on the charity and goodwill of their host, and in these circumstances the individual would, if they wished to survive, become adept at constantly sensing the changing and shifting currents, responding favourably to them, even, where possible exploiting them. For Edward, who had spent the greater part of his life (born *c.*1002, first exile 1013-1014, second exile 1016-1041) in this situation, it had become a way of life.

Thus we arrive at the first days of January 1066, England has an aged and ailing king who has not only failed to beget an heir, but who has in the course of his long reign promised the throne to his Norman cousin, allowed his elder half-brother's son and grandson to be brought back, if not quite into the fold of the English court at least back to England, elevated the throne worthy Earl of Wessex (his brother-in-law) to the position in all but name of 'mayor of the palace', and done nothing to refute the claims of the Kings of Denmark and Norway. Other candidates existed during the Confessor's reign, but by 1066 they were dead. We can also add to the list of dead, Edward the Exile. His son Edgar, Edmund Ironside's grandson, was however, still very much alive.

Neither Edward's failure in this crucial area of kingship, nor the plethora of candidates made the events of the succession crisis and thus Hastings inevitable. The final ingredient, the thing that set armies in motion and which led to three great battles and the death of two kings was the political situation in Europe:

... and he [Edward] passed away on the eve of Twelfth Night, and was buried on
Twelfth Night in the same minister ... However, the wise man [Edward again]
committed the kingdom to a distinguished man, Harold himself, a princely earl ...

Anglo-Saxon Chronicle C & D Mss., 1065

The funeral of the old king and the coronation of the new took place on the
same day, 6 January. The most throne worthy candidate and the heir of the House
of Cerdic, Edgar the Æthling, was passed over in favour of, if not a more worthy,
certainly a more powerful individual – Harold Godwinson, Earl of Wessex. The
passing of Edward marked, to all intents and purposes, the end of the Woden
descended Anglo-Saxon kings, whilst Harold II's *(colour plate 4)* accession saw,
as it turned out, the coronation of the last of the Anglo-Danish monarchs. For
Harold Godwinson was, albeit distantly via his mother, a member of the Danish
Royal House. His cousin, Swein Ulfsson (or Estrithson), King of Denmark, had
a better claim to the throne of England but he was neither then, nor for that
matter afterwards, in any real position to assert his claim.

Edward's death and Harold's seizure of the throne, as it was undoubtedly
viewed and indeed presented in some quarters, led to a flurry of military and
diplomatic activity. Stirring the pot (which needed little stirring) was Tostig, the
unfortunate former Earl of Northumbria and Harold's younger brother.

January, from Harold's point of view, was a bad time of year, possibly the worst,
to become king, as it gave anyone with a mind to intervene plenty of time to do
so. January 1066 was even worse, for the two contenders who entered the fray,
Harald Hardrada of Norway and William the Bastard of Normandy, were only
able to do so because of their respective stable political situations at home.

Hardrada based his claim to the throne on an agreement, a treaty, between
Harthacnut and Harald's predecessor Magnus. The treaty gave Magnus the
right to succeed to the throne of Denmark if Harthacnut predeceased him
(which of course he did). Therefore, in 1042 King Magnus the Good of
Norway invaded and took control of Denmark, he went further, however,
claiming, as did Harald after him, that the agreement with Harthacnut also
included England. Neither Magnus, nor Harald after him, were able to do
anything concrete regarding their claim as Denmark was far from secure. Over
the next 22 years Swein Ulfsson, who also claimed the throne of Denmark,
and had a claim to the throne of England on the death of Harthacnut, plotted,
fought and raided until in 1064 Harald finally sought peace. Swein may have
been left as king of Denmark but, as in 1042, he was in no position to challenge
for England. Denmark, his country was exhausted – two decades of warfare
had taken their toll.

Harald Hardrada, King of Norway, was according to William of Poitiers, "the most valiant warrior under heaven." He was, even though he lived at the end of the Age, the archetypal Viking – friends and enemies alike viewed him as a great warrior, he was bold, ruthless and certainly feared. He was also, as the events of 1066 show, a gambler (but then so were all the major players in the events of that year). In 1066 Norway, like Denmark, was drained. True it had never undergone a Danish invasion, but equally it had suffered loss and whilst it could be argued that Harald had not lost the war it was also true that he had not won it either. Harald's military prestige was thus not at an all-time high. Enter Tostig. Exiled in late 1065 Tostig had run poodle-like around the potentially interested courts of Europe trying to drum up support in order to facilitate his return to power in England as Earl of Northumbria. In Norway he found what he was looking for. It is impossible to say at this remove of time, particularly given the paucity of the sources, to say whether or not Hardrada would have intervened without Tostig's interference. Given the state of Norway, recovering from a long and protracted war he could have sat the succession crisis out, equally it was, as far as we can tell, in character to place the pursuit of *la gloire* above all else. Success in England would have removed the stain of the Danish campaigns and seen his military reputation reach new heights. The wealth of England would have allowed Harald to disavow his treaty with Swein, renew the war with Denmark and (hopefully) recreate Cnut's great northern empire – but this is of course speculation. But it was probably speculation that he weighed in his mind.

The other main candidate was William, called the Bastard, Duke of Normandy and cousin to Edward the Confessor. William's claim to the throne stemmed from a visit which the D or Worcester manuscript of the *Anglo-Saxon Chronicle* tells us that he made to England in 1051, shortly after the expulsion of the Godwin family. This was the zenith of Norman influence in Edwardian England. The Chronicle merely tells us that he was received by the king, yet it is likely that at this meeting Edward undertook the process of formalising William as his heir (for the time being). William, as later events would show, chose to take the matter as settled, Edward we suspect did not. The offer was not irreversible and was most likely made and formalised by Edward simply as part of his short-term management of the internal politics of his kingdom and as part of his then ongoing power struggle with his in-laws.

Further grist was added to William's mill by Harold's 1064 (this is the most likely year, although the exact date is not known) visit to Normandy. The Anglo-Saxon sources are silent on the subject of the visit, and even though the Norman sources disagree, the visit and its (for William's argument) all important oath – in which England's premier earl promised to support the Duke of Normandy's claim to the throne of England – undoubtedly took place.

What are we to make of Harold's (in)famous oath to William? Well Harold appears to have been rather profligate when it came to the swearing of oaths. Equally, as we lack the English sources and thus side of the argument, we are reduced to speculation, – Harold may well and probably did claim (and was in all fact) under duress at the time, in which case the oath, relics or no, was void. Harold also undoubtedly remembered his Shakespeare, in that – 'The better part of valour is discretion, in the which better part I have saved my life.' *The First Part of the History of Henry IV*, act 5, scene 4. In which case it was better to be forsworn and in England, than unsworn in Normandy.

The opening moves in the campaign of 1066 were diplomatic and astronomical. William of Normandy sent envoys to Harold (according to William of Jumièges) and to the Pontiff in Rome (according to William of Poitiers). The former rejected his claim, but the latter supported it. Astronomically, Halley's Comet 'appeared first on the eve of the *Greater Litany*, that is the 24 *April*, and shone thus all the week.' *Anglo-Saxon Chronicle* C ms. 1066. Signs are best read after the events they portend. Just as Wulfstan in his, *Sermon of 'Wolf' to the English when the Danes persecuted them most, which was in the year 1014 from the incarnation of our Lord Jesus Christ,* was able to say that the dreadful regicide of Edward the Martyr (amongst other things) inevitably brought the 'wrath of God' down onto the English, so the universal reading of disaster portended by the comet, became by the time of the post-conquest production of the Bayeux Tapestry, associated with the coronation and reign of Harold II.

The war turned hot at the beginning of May when Tostig arrived with 'as great a fleet as he could get' (*Anglo-Saxon Chronicle* D ms. 1066) off the Isle of Wight. The men of Wight bought Tostig off with money and provisions. Tostig then proceeded to raid along the South coast, eventually arriving at Sandwich. While Tostig was raiding, Harold in order to counter the real and more serious threat of William of Normandy, was in the process of raising a great army and fleet. Even before his preparations were complete he advanced on Sandwich and Tostig fled before him, taking with him in his flight (so the C manuscript of the *Anglo-Saxon Chronicle* informs us) some boatmen 'some willingly, some unwillingly.' Tostig next appeared in the Humber Estuary and from there raided Lindsey. However, here he was opposed by a force commanded by the Earls Edwin and Morcar (Earls of Mercia and Northumbria, respectively). The boatmen, according to the D text of the chronicle, also chose this moment to desert Tostig, and he again fled, this time with but twelve ships to Scotland and safety. It is hard to see, other than nuisance and disturbance, what Tostig hoped to gain or achieve. If he was hoping to repeat his father's success of the early 1050's then he was sadly deluded. In 1066 an English civil war was not a possibility, for at this time the Anglo-Saxon ruling elite had reached an accommodation and it most certainly did not include Tostig.

The host Harold assembled to counter William's threatened invasion was greater and more splendid than any yet seen in Britain since the end of the Roman period. The fleet assembled at Sandwich before moving with the king himself to the Isle of Wight. The army he deployed along the coast. Despite his grand preparations Harold was in a bit of a bind. Neither Harald's nor William's preparations could have been, nor indeed would have been, hidden. England's new king was therefore expecting to fight a war on two fronts, true he had forces in the north to deal with the Norwegian threat. But, and here's the rub, he did not know, within a narrow count of days when the assaults would come, nor could he know if by coincidence (for we are not looking at conspiracy) if he would face simultaneous or consecutive assaults, and if the latter dare he risk leaving a part of the country stripped of defence while he brought overwhelming force to bare, north or south, against an invader. Certainly it is unlikely that he hoped his great show of force would act as a deterrent. William by enlisting the blessing of the Pope and by persuading his own sceptical nobles to the cause, could not now back down without losing face, and that could have proved politically (and personally) fatal for him. Equally, Harald, who was viewed by many of his contemporaries as one of the greatest warriors of the age, was like William trapped by the heroic leadership constraints of the period.

The political situation in Scandinavia has already been considered. Turning now to Normandy the question needs to be asked – how was William in a position to launch such an enterprise?

To the English, after the great defeat, just as in the *Sermon of 'Wolf' to the English when the Danes persecuted them most, which was in the year 1014 from the incarnation of our Lord Jesus Christ,* death presaged foreign invasion and success, but to this matter we will return in due course. William's marriage to Matilda of Flanders, coupled with the exile of Tostig, who was the husband of Judith of Flanders, effectively removed Baldwin V, Count of Flanders and previously a supporter of the House of Godwin, from Harold's party in any forthcoming conflict. Equally the degree of hegemony that William had established over the lesser rulers to the north and west of his own territories, although important in helping to secure the frontiers of his duchy, was still not enough to ensure the safety of Normandy during the English venture given the large numbers of troops that he would have had to take within him in order to ensure a successful and credible assault. No, what really ensured William's safety, allowed him to persuade his nobles and to effectively strip his land of troops, were the deaths in 1060 of Henry I of France and Geoffrey of Anjou. These two rulers, when alive, had frequently warred against William. Had either (or both) been alive in 1066 then William's enterprise would have been far riskier, if not unattainable. Yet on their deaths they left minors as heirs and presented William, as it turned out, with a fortuitous window of opportunity. Even with this freedom of movement William could not act immediately. The King of Norway had ships, the Duke of Normandy did not, or at least not in the numbers required.

Harold's preparations were, as the Abingdon or C manuscript of the *Anglo-Saxon Chronicle* tells us, 'to no avail'. By the 8 September, the Nativity of St Mary, after having kept his forces in being and on station all through the Summer and Autumn, no attack had come and he was forced, as he could no longer hold them, to send his men back home and the fleet back to London. It is now impossible to say whether or not William and Harald, with their undoubted knowledge of the English military system, stayed their attack until after Harold was forced to disband his army, or that they attacked when they did because they were not ready earlier, or that Harold, using the administrative efficiency of the Anglo-Saxon State to the full had assembled his forces too early? The most plausible explanation is a combination of the second and the third reasons. Whatever the reason, or reasons, by the time the first of the main combatants entered the fray Harold's *Grande Armée* was no longer in being.

At some point between the 8 September (the Nativity of St Mary) and the 20 September, the Vigil of St Matthew the Apostle and the day on which the Battle of Fulford was fought, Harald Hardrada appeared at the mouth of the Tyne with 300 ships (*Anglo-Saxon Chronicle* E manuscript). Here he was joined by Tostig and together they followed the coast south until they came to the River Ouse. It may well be that Hardrada's invasion of the north of England was a deliberate attempt to replicate Swein Forkbeard's successful 1013 strategy. Entering the river they travelled upstream towards York, disembarking according to Simeon of Durham (who it must be noted supplies names for the landing site and subsequent battle) at Riccall, to the south of York. The landing at Riccall (Simeon's – Richale) probably took place on the 18 or 19 September. On the 20 September, a Wednesday and the Vigil of St Matthew the Apostle, at Fulford just outside and to the south of York, there was fought the decisive battle of the war.

The brother earls, Edwin of Mercia and Morcar of Northumbria have been criticised for engaging the enemy before Harold arrived with his southern army. Yet the criticism is political not military – with questions centring on the issue of – did the brothers attack in the hope that a victory would enhance their political power in the new regime? While it is possible that this was a consideration, the fact remains that the political settlement of 1065-66, which followed the expulsion of Tostig and the coronation of Harold II, saw a *rapprochement* between the houses of Godwin and Leofric, which left the latter in control of the midlands and the north. It saw their sister, Ealdgyth, married to the new king, Harold II, and thus the way opened for their nephew to, in the fullness of time, ascend to the throne of England as Harold III. The brothers were not noticeably lacking in political influence:

> Earl Edwin and Earl Morcar had gathered from their earldom as great a force as they could get, and fought with that raiding-army and made a great slaughter; and there many of the English people were killed and drowned and driven in flight; and the Norwegians had possession of the place of slaughter.

Anglo-Saxon Chronicle C manuscript, 1066

Simeon of Durham, in his entry for 1066, also tells us that the battle took place at Fulford on the north bank of the Ouse and that the English initially had the better of the contest before being overwhelmed by the Norwegians. Our sources are inconsistent on the subject of Harold's northward march. Some say that he marched north on hearing of the landing of Hardrada, others that news of the defeat galvanised him. In the scheme of things it actually matters little one way or the other. The decisiveness of Fulford lies in the fact of the English defeat, thereby necessitating Harold's northern march and the subsequent battle at Stamford Bridge.

Edwin and Morcar had to fight. They were charged with defending the north and midlands against foreign invasion, while the king guarded the south, and at Fulford that is precisely what they did, albeit unsuccessfully. There was no long road to the coronation of William, rather there were a series of events which with the benefit of hindsight can be turned into, and even give the appearance of an inevitable road. As it turned out some events were undoubtedly, inevitably, more important and decisive than others and in 1066 that honour belongs to the English defeat at Fulford. The reasons are all rather straightforward. An English victory would have meant that Harold's army would not have undergone two gruelling and exhausting forced marches with a battle and its inevitable casualties in between. Given the lateness of the Norman invasion there was now no hope of opposing the landing, however, an English victory at Fulford would have allowed Harold to field a larger and fresher army in the south than he was subsequently able to do. In either event it was unlikely that the Northumbrian and Mercian *fyrds* would have been involved, as it was Hardrada's victory appears to have knocked them out militarily, while a victory on the part of Edwin and Morcar would also in all probability have had little impact in the south as Harold was very likely to have engaged William before any northern force could have reached him. As it was, due to the failure of his brothers-in-law, Harold II of England was forced to march north to fight his renegade brother Tostig and Harald Hardrada of Norway.

Following the defeat, York submitted to the Norwegians handing over hostages and provisions (*83* and *84*). Yet success was fleeting, Hardrada was to be no Forkbeard, for Harold was no Aethelred. Five days after the battle on the Monday the 25 September 1066 there occurred one of the greatest feats of Anglo-Saxon arms. Harold II's forced march north has been described as brilliant and lightening fast, and these assessments are fair, for in military terms he achieved that rarest of things – strategic surprise. The English caught the Norwegians completely unawares at Stamford Bridge to the north-east of York. The C ms. tells us that Harald and Tostig where at Stamford Bridge awaiting more hostages, instead they found themselves facing a hostile force. According to Snorri Sturluson, *Heimskringla* (*The Saga of Harald Sigurtharson (Hardruler)*, 91), there was an absolutely marvellous conversation between the two estranged brothers immediately prior to the start of the battle in the course of which King Harold offered Harald Hardrada 'seven feet of English soil or so much more as he is taller than other men.' Did such a conversation occur? To answer that question (or possibly to side-step it) I would suggest that you watch that great film *The man who shot Liberty Valance*. The conversation is, however, reminiscent of a meeting between Hannibal and Scipio before the Battle of Zama, although Polybius is a far better and more reliable historian than Snorri Sturluson.

In the ensuing battle the English overwhelmed the unprepared Norwegians and utterly defeated them, gaining in the process what has been viewed as the most complete victory ever achieved by the English over Vikings. Although it could be argued that it shares that honour with Athelstan's great victory at Brunanburh in AD 937. According to the D manuscript of the *Anglo-Saxon Chronicle* the English pursued the remnants of the Norwegian force to their ships. At the end of the battle and pursuit our sources say that the surviving Norwegians could man but 24 ships (*Anglo-Saxon Chronicle* D ms.), Florence of Worcester puts the figure at 20 ships. Either way a truly decisive English victory. Harald Hardrada and Tostig perished in the battle.

Harold's victory quickly turned to ash in his mouth, for on the 28 September William of Normandy with his host landed in England. Initially at Pevensey where he began the raising of a castle. However, the next day (29 September) he rapidly moved down the coast to Hastings and there raised a second castle.

Before, however, we move south one final question needs answering about Harold II's army at Stamford Bridge – was a part of the English force shipborne? The answer is probably, no. The Abingdon or C manuscript of the *Anglo-Saxon Chronicle* uses the term *lith* to describe a part of the English army at Tadcaster prior to the Battle of Stamford Bridge. In this context *lith* should be taken to mean the personnel of (or at least a part of the men who manned) the English fleet which was based in London and who, if we are to read C correctly, formed a part of the army which Harold led north.

Above: 83 York, despite its great defences (see *84*) capitulated, without siege, to Harald Hardrada at the Battle of Fulford.

Left: 84 The Multangular Tower at York. Roman with later additions, it originally formed a part of the defences of the legionary fortress, but was later incorporated into the Anglian, Viking and Medieval defences of the city.

… we now understood what work lay before us, and with the help of our Lord Jesus Christ must conquer in all battles and engagements. We must be properly prepared, he [Cortes] said, for each one of them, because if we were at any time defeated, which God forbid, we should not be able to raise our heads again, being so few. He added that we could look for no help or assistance except from God … . Therefore we must rely on our own good swords and stout hearts.

Bernal Díaz, *The Conquest of New Spain*

William's planned invasion was a gamble, he knew it and his nobles knew it, indeed according to William of Poitiers they pointed it out to him. Yet time and events were on William's side, for as has already been pointed out the death of Edward so early in the year gave the rival claimants room to manoeuvre. Diplomatically, for William, the Pope's blessing would only be of value if he won, although in morale terms the papal banner would potentially be of benefit on the field of battle. What the time really gave him was a chance to construct a fleet, hire mercenaries and attack that very year, before Harold's position became too well entrenched, and before he perhaps lost (through unforeseen circumstances) his continental window of opportunity. William was also in the fortunate position of being able to incentivise noble and mercenary alike with the promise of rich rewards if they succeeded − England was after all a wealthy well-ordered polity. Thus risk and reward went hand-in-hand with concomitant high levels of each.

Harold, aware of these preparations, and unable to prevent the Norman recruitment drive, does seem to have launched a spoiling attack against his enemy's burgeoning invasion fleet. The attack which is mentioned in the E manuscript of the *Anglo-Saxon Chronicle* and in *Little Domesday* (Essex VI. Hundred of Ongar) does not appear to have been a success. Prior to concentration and the boarding of the army, the Norman fleet was probably too widely dispersed for a single raid to have much effect.

William's 'mad proceedings' finally got under way, it is thought, on the 27 September. It also appears to show from the timing of events that William was aware of the other major players and that he timed his departure to coincide with Harold's re-mobilisation and march north. William seems to have sought the added security of landing on an undefended, if not an unwatched, coast. William landed at Pevensey (and began the raising of a castle) on the eve of the Feast of St Michael. His initial landing appears to have been further west than planned, for the next day, the feast day itself, he moved to Hastings and there raised a second castle. Alongside defence William's other overriding concern was food. The Bayeux Tapestry presents this living off the land as foraging, to the English it was pillaging.

It may also have been designed, particularly as the depredations were on Harold's patrimony, to prompt the king into a hasty and ill-considered action. For not only was the England that Harold had sworn to defend under attack (it must be remembered that a king was the shield of his people – see for example *Beowulf* lines 1866ff.), but his own tenants were baring the brunt of the attack.

Various reasons have at times been advanced as to why William did not march inland. The reason that he did not, was that his prime concern were his lines of communication. He needed to find, engage, and defeat Harold. He was, however, constrained. As with the Achaeans before the walls of Troy, so to with William, the defence of the ships was paramount. Thus any battle fought must be fought near Hastings, for if anything went wrong (and well it might) then the fleet remained his only hope of escape. Equally, a march inland may well have left the fleet vulnerable to attack and destruction. True, William was, as time went on, in a position to slowly increase the range of his depredations, but there were limits, albeit self imposed ones based upon the necessity of ensuring the security of the fleet. A secondary consideration, which may have weighed with William, was that not only may these attacks on Harold's own land have the effect of precipitating rash action, but by staying in one place he drew the king to him and thus to an extent controlled the course of events. Possibly by forcing battle on his own timetable and on land which he, William, had personally reconnoitred, although in this respect it must be remembered that Hastings was no Austerlitz, and Senlac was not the Pratzen Heights.

In terms of timetables we have very few fixed dates. We do not know when Harold heard of William's landing, nor do we know for that matter where he received the fateful news. Florence of Worcester tells us explicitly (the *Anglo-Saxon Chronicle* E ms. implicitly) that he spent some time (but maybe not enough) in London, leaving on or around the 11 October. Harold has been criticised for the length of time he spent in London, usually on the grounds that it was not long enough, yet how valid is such criticism? Controversy and criticism centres on the size of the host that Harold led out of London to Hastings. Although it must be admitted that the debate centres around relatives rather than absolutes. Equally, some claims concerning the quality of parts of the English force do not even rise to the level of specious – the view that Harold's army contained club armed peasants is just plain wrong – both sides at Hastings, indeed in all the battles of 1066 (and before), consisted of experienced, professional warriors armed and equipped with the latest in military technology. Returning to the London question. Harold's kingship still required validation, certainly so far he had been no slouch, the victory over Hardrada showed that, however, in order to set the seal on all that he had achieved (the crown, the political accommodation, his marriage) he needed to show the English people that he was emphatically the right man in the right place and in order to do that he had to drive William back into the sea.

William of Poitiers tells us that Harold, possibly in a repeat of his successful 1063 Welsh strategy, dispatched a giant fleet with the intention of attacking the Normans from the sea. If this were so then Harold could not have tarried too long in London, as such a strategy would only have worked if co-ordinated to coincide with a land attack, and given the lateness of the year, in terms of weather conditions, the sooner such a venture was launched the better. As to the size of his host, Harold had to weigh the extra men he would have received by sitting in London for longer, against the damage done to his reputation and his patrimony by William's foragers. In the end, like Byrhtnoth some 70 years earlier, he undoubtedly reasoned that he already had the numbers to do the job, waiting would have served little purpose and swiftness had served him well in the past. Also had not this same army not just beaten the greatest warrior in the Northern world and won one of the most decisive victories in Anglo-Saxon history. Morale, Harold would have reasoned, goes along way towards winning battles. Harold therefore probably rode out of London at the head of his army with high hopes, he was to be disappointed.

On the morning of the 14 October in the year of the Lord 1066 Harold of England failed to surprise William of Normandy.

Of course Harold (85) may have intended simply to fight a defensive battle using some suitable piece of terrain to counter William's cavalry supremacy, or he could have intended to bottle the Normans up in Hastings. We simply do not know what Harold planned. What we do know is that the English army was seen by William's pickets, the Duke forewarned was therefore able to assemble his army and march out to meet his enemy. We cannot now, at this remove and with the available evidence, reconstruct Harold's original plan, however, the position which he occupied, Senlac ridge, astride the London road, was an excellent defensive position. His flanks were secured by the terrain and his enemy was forced to attack uphill, which William promptly did.

The battle began at around 9a.m. ("the third hour of the day" according to Simeon of Durham). William's archers attempted to soften-up the English as a prelude to an infantry attack. Neither the archers nor the infantry made any impression on the English line and William was therefore forced to turn to his cavalry. Riding uphill is not a problem (see for example Xenophon *On the Art of Horsemanship*, VIII.8), riding uphill into steady, formed, close-order infantry with secure flank is, as the Normans soon found out. Horses make easy and inviting targets for long spears. The attack failed utterly, in fact it failed to the extent that it provoked the first real crisis of the day and placed victory within Harold's grasp. Yet as we know it slipped through his fingers — the question is why?

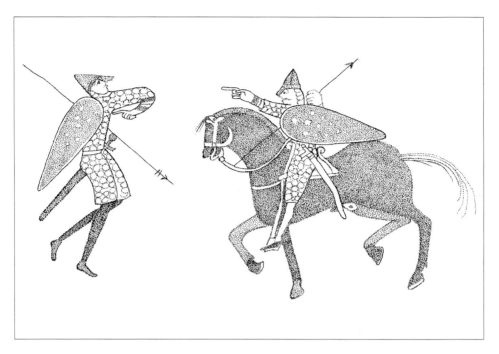

85 Harold II, mounted, and a scout/messenger, from the Bayeux Tapestry.

The cavalry failed to either overawe or penetrate the English position, rather it appears from William of Poitiers that the 'ferocity' and skill of the English caused such a slaughter that the retreat of the cavalry became panicky. As if the knights wished to get themselves and their horses (the main target due to their size and lack of armour) away from the spears and broad axes of the defenders on the hill top. It appears to have been at this point that a rumour spread that William was dead, and this nearly proved disastrous for the Norman cause. Thus what started simply as a disorderly retreat by the Bretons on William's left flank, quickly, on the receipt of this news, spread to the whole army:

> Somebody shouted 'Now's the time, my boys,' and the Guards leaped forward with their bayonets, over the gruesome barrier of corpses.

> Howarth, 1968, *Waterloo: A Near Run Thing*

Now was indeed Harold's time, his position on the hill top would have given him an excellent view of the chaos in the enemy's ranks. The Normans and their allies (mercenaries) would not stand, a general advance would have won him the battle – all he needed to do was give the order.

86 An English standard bearer and a housecarl, from the
Bayeux Tapestry.

Opinion over the English counter-attack differs. Douglas in his work on
William the Conqueror believes that Harold failed to order such an attack and
thus missed his chance of victory. Morillo, on the other-hand, is of the view that
he did order an attack and that it was commanded by the king's brothers, the Earls
Gyrth and Leofwine. I tend to support Morillo, I believe that Harold did order
a counter-attack. I also, however, believe that crucially, and for the English cause
fatally, that he hedged his bets. For at this point a general advance by the whole
of the English army would probably have decided the issue, it would have won
the battle for Harold and ended permanently the Norman conquest. However,
what seems to have happened is that a partial, albeit large scale counter-attack
was ordered by Harold, most likely under the command of his brothers Gyrth
and Leofwine. They were to sweep away the enemy, while he, Harold, remained
on the ridge with the lesser part of the host, which would have acted as a rallying
point were the English attack to fail (*86* and *colour plate 3*).

The English attack did fail and it appears, as Morillo suggests, to have failed at
the very outset, probably as a result of the deaths of Gyrth and Leofwine. Their
sudden demise in the forefront of the attack stalled the centre of the line but
not the wings. The former, mostly, reformed on the ridge, the latter continued
to advance. William was of course not dead and the confusion and hesitation in
the English ranks gave him the time to rally and steady his troops. The apparent
failure of the Anglo-Saxons to launch a co-ordinated assault presented William

87 Lesser thegns in combat at Hastings, on the Bayeux Tapestry.

with an opportunity, which he took. The individuals and scattered groups who had advanced were now overrun and slaughtered by the cavalry of the Normans and their allies. Some will have made it back to the ridge, where the English in all probability redressed their line.

The moment was passed, crisis averted, neither side had lost, equally neither side had won:

> Then an unusual kind of combat ensued, one side attacking in bursts and in a variety of movements, the other rooted in the ground, putting up with the assault.

William of Poitiers, *Gesta Willelmi*

The failure of the English counter-attack appears to have trapped Harold on his ridge. He lacked the numbers to resume the offensive, nor was he in a position to break-off the engagement, as such a movement would have spelt doom for the English as the Norman horse would have pursued them through the long day. However, the situation was not that bleak, it was true that offence and retreat were ruled out, but for Harold a draw would suffice, there were no Prussians to come but there was night. All the English had to do was to hold fast on the ridge until dusk called a halt to proceedings. Harold and his army could then slip away, regroup, re-enforce, and return to face William another day. For William such an outcome would have been disastrous. As the year waned and winter took hold his lines of communication would become increasingly tenuous. William needed a decisive victory.

The remainder of the battle became a struggle of attrition. The Normans with little success appear to have launched attack after attack against the English. As for the feigned flights, they probably occurred, and their success may be attributed to frustration on the part of some of the English army. Generally, however, this phase shows rather the quality of the Anglo-Saxon infantry in that they were able to beat off attack after attack for hours on end, all through what must have seemed an interminable afternoon. Infantry was proving more than a match for cavalry (87 and *colour plate 2*).

The battle was decided, and as it turned out the fate of the kingdom with it, by tactical asymmetry.

The long period from the death of Edward the Confessor to the departure of the Norman fleet gave William ample time to recruit. The promised rewards were high and one of the results of this potential largesse was the fact that William was able to field a far greater force of archers than was normal for a Duke of Normandy. William of Poitiers alludes to the punishment inflicted on the English by the Norman archers throughout the afternoon of the battle, and this it was that won him the day.

The final Norman assault of the day, like the first, was preceded by the Norman archers again attempting to soften-up the English − this time they succeeded. Harold's army had done much that it could be proud of, both in the campaign as a whole and in the days fighting outside Hastings, yet the advantages of asymmetry were telling against it. The enemy's superiority in archers had taken its toll and the indomitable shield wall was now reduced to a position where it may not have been able to withstand another assault. William needed this final assault to succeed, and at this point fate or luck intervened on the Norman part. Harold was mortally wounded in the eye by an arrow. With his brothers already dead, along with so many others, the leadership, and the morale of the English collapsed. The mental collapse was rapidly followed by the physical collapse of the English shield wall in the face of the final Norman assault of the day. Harold died by his standard, cut to pieces. The death of Harold and the English defeat proved what William had always maintained, that God was on his side and the crown was rightfully his. The coming of night and the probable exhaustion of the Norman and their allies, curtailed the pursuit.

The death of Harold was a crushing psychological blow from which the English elite never recovered. One suspects that the death of the king in battle at Hastings was viewed in the same light as the return of the Vikings during the reign of Aethelred − namely as God's judgement upon the sinful English. Whatsoever was the case, the paralysis at what was left of the top of English

88 The end of the world. The castle motte, York, one of many constructed by William, now the Conqueror, to help secure and solidify his rule.

society (three battles in so short a space of time had taken their toll on the elite) allowed William complete freedom of action.

In this time of crisis the English looked to the certainties of the past and to the House of Cerdic. Edgar, the grandson of Edmund Ironside, and the great-grandson of Aethelred II, was declared king. Yet this attempt to curry divine favour, as Higham sees it, did little if anything to bolster English morale. Dover capitulated without siege and despite the great force of well-armed men that William of Poitiers believes that the English possessed in London, nothing seems to have been done to raise a new field army to counter the Norman threat. For the Anglo-Saxon State and Edgar's regime to survive, dynamic military action was required. Such action singularly failed to materialise. Edwin and Morcar, who probably acted as the war leaders for the new young king, effectively sat on their hands.

William, recognising the opportunity presented to him by the death of Harold and his great victory, acted decisively and brutally.

> ... he [William] went inland with all of his raiding-army which was left to him and [what] came to him afterwards from across the sea, and raided all that region he travelled across until he came to Berkhamsted.
>
> *Anglo-Saxon Chronicle* D manuscript, 1066

William used ravaging as a weapon of terror and intimidation. The sole English attempt to interdict William and to try to dent the perception of Norman invincibility which had developed since Hastings, ended in disaster. A foray by Edgar's London forces, launched when William reached Southwark, ended in the defeat of the English. To further compound the English failure William burnt Southwark – the smoke of the burning undoubtedly cast a depressing pall over the city. The final straw came when William arrived at Berkhamsted and placed his army astride one of the main routes between London and the West Midlands. Edgar's regime had failed and all that was left to do was to submit to William. William the Bastard, Duke of Normandy and cousin of the late king of noble memory, Edward the Confessor, was crowned King of England on Midwinter's Day 1066 by Archbishop Aldred of York, in Westminster Abbey (*88*).

William won because Harold died. Had Harold survived then we would have been into a whole different kettle of fish. Yet crucially and critically that death, coming on top of everything else that had occurred since the death of Edward at the beginning of the year destroyed the will of the ruling elite. Armies were there to be raised against the invader, however, a fatal paralysis had set in at the top. The War of the English Succession was both a political and a military matter. Politics gained Harold the throne and warfare, up to a point, helped him secure it, that point came in the closing hours of the Battle of Hastings when his luck ran out. Harold was a good general with a good army, and apart from his probable hedging over the English counter-attack at Hastings he appears to have been bold and decisive. In the final analysis circumstances; particularly Edwin and Morcar's failure to defeat Harald Hardrada, as well as the asymmetry of the forces at Hastings; told against him. Plus, finally, fatally his luck ran out, and that was important, for as both Frederick the Great and Napoleon are said to have observed on being appraised of an officer's record:

Yes, yes, I know he's brilliant – but is he lucky?

APPENDIX

DESCRIPTION OF COLOUR RECONSTRUCTIONS

RECONSTRUCTION 1 – BYRHTNOTH AT MALDON, AD 991

The helmet is a simple, single-piece example based upon the find from Hradsko in Bohemia. The spear is a common winged Carolingian type, the javelins are typical late Viking examples and are tanged rather than socketed. The mail shirt is based upon a number of contemporary Anglo-Saxon manuscript illustrations. The sword is from Hedeby and has been dated between the tenth and elevnth century. The seax is based upon a number of extant examples, and the scabbard is from York, the seax suspension method is conjectural. The shield is taken from the picture of Goliath in British Library, *Ms. Cotton Tiberius C VI*. The spurs are from Brandstrup, central Jutland.

RECONSTRUCTION 2 – LESSER THEGN, C. AD 1066

The helmet is again eastern being from Gnezdovo and is now in the State Historical Museum, Moscow. His axe is from Fyrkat, while his spear is taken from a Viking example in the British Museum. The reverse of his kite-shield shows one possible suspension/grip method. His Petersen type Z sword is Finnish.

RECONSTRUCTION 3 – HOUSECARL, C. AD 1066

The typical Norman style helmet is the Olmütz helmet from Moravia. His mail shirt, including the method of sword suspension is taken primarily from the Bayeux Tapestry, but this style is also seen in other works of the period, see for example the early twelfth-century images of Goliath in Santa Maria de Tahull, Catalonia. The ventail interpretation of the Bayeux Tapestry chest-square is preferred and therefore appears here and in reconstruction 4. The broad axe is one of the London Bridge finds. The Petersen type Xa sword is taken from a Finnish example.

Reconstruction 4 – King Harold II, Godwinson, ad 1066

This reconstruction is based upon an image of the king in the Bayeux Tapestry, and shows Harold as the epitome of an eleventh-century European warrior aristocrat. He is wearing the St Wenceslas helmet, his sword is from Lough Derg, County Tipperary, while his spearhead is Finnish.

SELECT BIBLIOGRAPHY

The following bibliography lists the main, and at times the most easily accessible secondary works, used in researching this subject. These secondary sources themselves contain bibliographies, which spread the net, so to speak. In terms of primary sources, the Swanton translations of the *Anglo-Saxon Chronicle* and *Beowulf*, and Scragg's translation of *The Battle of Maldon*, are preferred, but not exclusively so, to other translations. Bradley's *Anglo-Saxon Poetry* and Whitelock's *English Historical Documents c.500-1042* (2nd edition) have also proved invaluable. As has Ashdown's *English and Norse Documents relating to the reign of Ethelred the Unready*. The Stevenson translations of the histories of both Florence of Worcester and Simeon of Durham have been used. Both the *Encomium Emmae Reginae* (Campbell and Keynes) and *The Life of King Edward the Confessor* (Barlow) have been used; however, they are more valuable as political as opposed to military sources. In the case of the classical works cited the Loeb translations of these authors are used.

Abels, R.P., *Lordship and Military Obligation in Anglo-Saxon England* (London, 1998).

Abels, R.P. and Bachrach, B.S. (eds), *The Normans and Their Adversaries at War: Essays in Memory of C. Warren Hollister* (Woodbridge, 2001).

Aitchison, N., *The Picts and the Scots at War* (Stroud, 2003).

Arnold, T., *The Renaissance at War* (London, 2001).

Backhouse, J., Turner, D.H. and Webster, L., *The Golden Age of Anglo-Saxon Art 966-1066* (London, 1984).

Bailey, R.N., *Viking Age Sculpture in Northern England* (London, 1980).

Barlow, F., *Edward the Confessor* (London, 1970).

Barlow, F., *The Godwins*, (Harlow, 2002).

Bennett, M., *Campaigns of the Norman Conquest* (Oxford, 2001).

Bradbury, J., *The Medieval Archer* (Woodbridge, 1985).

Bradbury, J., *The Battle of Hastings* (Stroud, 1998).

Brooks, N., *Communities and Warfare 700-1400* (London, 2000).

Cameron, E.A., *Sheaths and Scabbards in England AD 400-1100* (Oxford, 2000).

Christensen, A.E. (ed.), *The Earliest Ships: The Evolution of Boats into Ships* (London, 1996).

Cooper, J. (ed.), *The Battle of Maldon: Fiction and Fact* (London, 1993).

Davidson, H.R.E., *The Sword in Anglo-Saxon England: Its Archaeology and Literature* (Woodbridge, 1962).

Davies, S., *Welsh Military Institutions 633-1283* (Cardiff, 2004).

DeVries, K., *The Norwegian Invasion of England in 1066* (Woodbridge, 1999).

Dickinson, T. and Härke, H., *Early Anglo-Saxon Shields* (London, 1992).

Evans, S.S., *The Lords of Battle: Image and Reality of the Comitatus in Dark-Age Britain* (Woodbridge, 1997).

Falk, H., *Altnordische Waffenkunde* (Kristiania, 1914).

Falkner, J., *Great and Glorious Days: Marlborough's Battles 1704-09* (Staplehurst, 2002).

Fletcher, I (ed.), *The Peninsular War: Aspects of the Struggle for the Iberian Peninsular* (Staplehurst, 1998).

Forte, A., Oram, R. and Pedersen, F., *Viking Empires* (Cambridge, 2005).

France, J., *Victory in the East: A Military History of the First Crusade* (Cambridge, 1994).

France, J., *Western Warfare in the Age of the Crusades 1000-1300* (London, 1999).

Gaebel, R.E., *Cavalry Operations in the Ancient Greek World* (Norman, 2002).

Goldsworthy, A.K., *The Roman Army at War 100 BC-AD200* (Oxford, 1996).

Gravett, C., *Hastings 1066: The Fall of Saxon England* (Oxford, 1992).

Gravett, C., *Norman Knight 950-1204 AD* (London, 1993).

Grieg, S., *Gjermundbufunnet* (Oslo, 1947).

Griffith, P., *The Viking Art of War* (London, 1995).

Haldon, J., *The Byzantine Wars: Battles and Campaigns of the Byzantine Era* (Stroud, 2001).

Halsall, G., *Warfare and Society in the Barbarian West, 450-900* (London, 2003).

Hanson, V.D., *The Western Way of War: Infantry Battle in Classical Greece* (Oxford, 1990).

Hanson, V.D. (ed.), *Hoplites: The Classical Greek Battle Experience* (London, 1991).

Hardy, R., *The Longbow: A Social and Military History* (Sparkford, 1976).

Harris, V., *Cutting Edge: Japanese Swords in the British Museum* (London, 2004).

Harrison, M., *Viking Hersir 793-1066AD* (London, 1993).

Hawkes, S.C. (ed.), *Weapons and Warfare in Anglo-Saxon England* (Oxford, 1989).

Higham, N.J., *The Death of Anglo-Saxon England* (Stroud, 1997).

Hollister, C.W., *Anglo-Saxon Military Institutions on the Eve of the Norman Conquest* (Oxford, 1962).

Howard, I., *Swein Forkbeard's Invasion and the Danish Conquest of England, 991-1017* (Woodbridge, 2003).

Howarth, D., *Waterloo: A Near Run Thing* (Glasgow, 1968).

Howarth, D., *1066: The Year of the Conques* (1977).

John, E., *Land Tenure in Early England: A Discussion of Some Problems* (Leicester, 1964).

John, E., *Orbis Britanniae and Other Studies* (Leicester, 1966).

John, E., *Reassessing Anglo-Saxon England* (Manchester, 1996).

Jones, C., *The Forgotten Battle of 1066 Fulford* (Stroud, 2006).

Jørgensen, A.N. and Clausen, B.L., *Military Aspects of Scandinavian Society in a European Perspective, AD 1-1300* (Copenhagen, 1997).

Jørgensen, A.N., Pind, J., Jørgensen, L. and Clausen, B. (eds), *Maritime Warfare in Northern Europe: Technology, Organisation, Logistics and Administration 500 BC-1500 AD* (Copenhagen, 2002).

Jörgensen, C. (et al.), *Fighting Techniques of the Early Modern World AD 1500-AD 1763: Equipment, Combat Skills and Tactics* (Staplehurst, 2005).

Kagay, D.J. and Villalon, L.J.A. (eds), *The Circle of War in the Middle Ages: Essays on Medieval Military and Naval History* (Woodbridge, 1999).

Kendrick, T.D., *Late Saxon and Viking Art* (London, 1949).

Lavelle, R., *Aethelred II: King of the English 978-1016* (Stroud, 2002).

Lawson, M.K., *Cnut: The Danes in England in the Early Eleventh Century* (London, 1993).

Lawson, M.K., *The Battle of Hastings 1066* (Stroud, 2002).

Lendon, J.E., *Soldiers and Ghosts: A History of Battle in Classical Antiquity* (New Haven, 2005).

Leppäaho, J., *Späteisenzeitliche Waffen aus Finnland* (Helsinki, 1964).

Lindholm, D. and Nicolle, D., *Medieval Scandinavian Armies (1) 1100-1300* (Oxford, 2003).

McGeer, E., *Sowing the Dragon's Teeth: Byzantine Warfare in the Tenth Century* (Washington D.C., 1995).

Morillo, S., *Warfare under the Anglo-Norman Kings 1066-1135* (Woodbridge, 1994).

Morillo, S. (ed.), *The Battle of Hastings: Sources and Interpretations* (Woodbridge, 1996).

Nafziger, G., *Imperial Bayonets: Tactics of the Napoleonic Battery, Battalion and Brigade as Found in Contemporary Regulations* (London, 1996).

Nicolle, D., *Arthur and the Anglo-Saxon Wars* (London, 1984).

Nicolle, D., *Arms and Armour of the Crusading Era 1050-1350*, 2 vols. (Woodbridge, 1999).

Nicolle, D., *Armies of Medieval Russia 750-1250*, (Oxford, 1999).

Nicolle, D., *Carolingian Cavalryman AD 768-987* (Oxford, 2005).

Oakeshott, E., *The Archaeology of Weapons: Arms and Armour from Prehistory to the Age of Chivalry* (London, 1960).

Oakeshott, E., *The Sword in the Age of Chivalry* (Woodbridge, 1994).

Oman, C., *A History of the Art of War in the Middle Ages 378-1485AD*, 2 vols. (London, 1924).

Owen-Crocker, G.R. (ed.), *King Harold II and the Bayeux Tapestry* (Woodbridge, 2005).

Petersen, J., *Die Norske Vikingesverd* (Kristiania, 1919).

Peirce, I., *Swords of the Viking Age* (Woodbridge, 2002).

Powicke, M., *Military Obligation in Medieval England* (Oxford, 1962).

Pullen-Appleby, J., *English Sea Power c871 to 1100* (Hockwold-cum-Wilton, 2005).

Richards, J., *Landsknecht Soldier 1486-1560* (Oxford, 2002).

Rodger, N.A.M., *The Safeguard of the Sea: A Naval History of Britain Volume One 660-1649* (London, 1997).

Rose, S., *Medieval Naval Warfare 1000-1500* (London, 2002).

Sawyer, P. (ed.), *The Oxford Illustrated History of the Vikings* (Oxford, 1997).

Scragg, D. (ed.), *The Battle of Maldon AD 991* (Oxford, 1991).

Scragg, D., *The Return of the Vikings: The Battle of Haldon 991* (Stroud, 2006).

Shetelig, H., Falk, H. and Gordon, E.V., *Scandinavian Archaeology* (Oxford, 1937).

Snodgrass, A.M., *Arms and Armour of the Greeks* (Baltimore, 1999).

Stafford, P., *Unification and Conquest: A Political and Social History of England in the Tenth and Eleventh Centuries* (London, 1989).

Starkey, D., *Elizabeth: Apprenticeship* (London, 2000).

Starkey, D., *The Monarchy of England: The Beginnings* (London, 2004).

Stenton, F. (ed.), *The Bayeux Tapestry: A Comprehensive Survey* (London, 1957).

Stephenson, I.P., *Roman Infantry Equipment: The Later Empire* (Stroud, 1999).

Stephenson, I.P., *The Anglo-Saxon Shield* (Stroud, 2002).

Stephenson, I.P., *Romano-Byzantine Infantry Equipment* (Stroud, 2006).

Strickland, M. (ed.), *Anglo-Norman Warfare: Studies in Late Anglo-Saxon and Anglo-Norman Military Organization and Warfare* (Woodbridge, 1992).

Strickland, M. and Hardy, R., *The Great Warbow: From Hastings to the Mary Rose* (Stroud, 2005).

Swanton, M.J., *The Spearheads of the Anglo-Saxon Settlements* (London, 1973).

Syvänne, I., *The Age of Hippotoxotai: Art of War in Roman Military Revival and Disaster (491-636)* (Tampere, 2004).

Tweddle, D., *The Anglian Helmet from Coppergate* (York, 1992).

Underwood, R., *Anglo-Saxon Weapons and Warfare* (Stroud, 1999).

van Wees, H. 2004: *Greek Warfare: Myths and Realities*, (London, 2004).

Wheeler, R.E.M., *London and the Vikings* (London, 1927).

Whitelock, D., *The Beginnings of English Society: The Anglo-Saxon Period* (Harmondsworth, 1952).

Wilson, D.M., *Anglo-Saxon Art: from the Seventh Century to the Norman Conquest*, London, 1984).

Wilson, D.M., *The Bayeux Tapestry* (London, 1985).

INDEX